CO-OPS AND CONDOMINIUMS: YOUR RIGHTS AND OBLIGATIONS AS AN OWNER

by
Margaret C. Jasper

Oceana's Legal Almanac Series:
Law for the Layperson

2005
Oceana Publications, Inc.
Dobbs Ferry, New York

You may order this or any Oceana publication by visiting Oceana's website at http://www.oceanalaw.com

Library of Congress Control Number: 2005925300

ISBN 0-379-11395-3

Oceana's Legal Almanac Series: Law for the Layperson
ISSN 1075-7376

©2005 by Oceana Publications, Inc.

Manufactured in the United States of America on acid-free paper.

To My Husband Chris

Your love and support
are my motivation and inspiration

-and-

In memory of my son, Jimmy

Table of Contents

CHAPTER 8:
THE PLANNED COMMUNITY

APPENDICES

ABOUT THE AUTHOR

MARGARET C. JASPER is an attorney engaged in the general practice of law in South Salem, New York, concentrating in the areas of personal injury and entertainment law. Ms. Jasper holds a Juris Doctor degree from Pace University School of Law, White Plains, New York, is a member of the New York and Connecticut bars, and is certified to practice before the United States District Courts for the Southern and Eastern Districts of New York, the United States Court of Appeals for the Second Circuit, and the United States Supreme Court.

Ms. Jasper has been appointed to the panel of arbitrators of the American Arbitration Association and the law guardian panel for the Family Court of the State of New York, is a member of the Association of Trial Lawyers of America, and is a New York State licensed real estate broker and member of the Westchester County Board of Realtors, operating as Jasper Real Estate, in South Salem, New York. Margaret Jasper maintains a website at http://www.JasperLawOffice.com.

Ms. Jasper is the author and general editor of the following legal almanacs: AIDS Law; The Americans with Disabilities Act; Animal Rights Law; The Law of Attachment and Garnishment; Bankruptcy Law for the Individual Debtor; Individual Bankruptcy and Restructuring; Banks and their Customers; Buying and Selling Your Home; The Law of Buying and Selling; The Law of Capital Punishment; The Law of Child Custody; Your Rights in a Class Action Suit; Commercial Law; Consumer Rights Law; The Law of Contracts; Copyright Law; Credit Cards and the Law; The Law of Debt Collection; Dictionary of Selected Legal Terms; The Law of Dispute Resolution; Drunk Driving Law; DWI, DUI and the Law; Education Law; Elder Law; Employee Rights in the Workplace; Employment Discrimination Under Title VII; Environmental Law; Estate Planning; Everyday Legal Forms; Executors and Personal Representatives: Rights and Responsibilities; Harassment in the Workplace; Health Care and Your Rights. Home Mortgage Law Primer; Hospital Liability Law; Identity Theft and How To Protect Yourself; Insurance Law; The Law of Immigration; International Adoption; Juvenile Justice and Children's Law; Labor Law; Landlord-Tenant Law; The Law of Libel and Slander; Living Together: Practical Legal Issues; Marriage and Divorce; The Law of Medical Malpractice; Motor Vehicle Law; The Law of No-Fault Insurance; Nursing Home Negligence; The Law of Obscenity and Pornography; Patent Law; The Law of Personal Injury; The Law of Premises Liability; Prescription Drugs; Privacy and the Internet: Your Rights and Expectations Under the Law; Probate Law; The Law of Product Liability; Real Estate Law for the Homeowner and Broker; Religion and the Law; Retirement Planning; The Right to Die; Rights of Single Parents; Law for the Small Business Owner; Small Claims Court; Social Security Law; Special Education Law; The Law of Speech and the First Amendment; Teenagers and Substance Abuse; Trademark Law; Victim's Rights Law; The Law of Violence Against Women; Welfare: Your Rights and the Law; What if it Happened to You: Violent Crimes and Victims' Rights; What if the Product Doesn't Work: Warranties & Guarantees; Workers' Compensation Law; and Your Child's Legal Rights: An Overview.

INTRODUCTION

Many people use the words co-op and condo interchangeably, when referring to a dwelling which is neither a rental apartment nor a privately-owned single family home. In fact, some state statutes refer to co-ops and condos jointly as common interest communities. However, there is a major difference between the two. It is not the type of property that makes the difference, but the type of ownership of the property.

This almanac discusses the differences between co-op and condo ownership, the rights and obligations of the respective owners, and financing and insurance issues. The development of the planned community—another form of common interest community—is also explored. This almanac also examines conversion—the process by which a rental property becomes a co-op or condominium.

The Appendix provides resource directories, statutes and other pertinent information and data. The Glossary contains definitions of many of the terms used throughout the almanac.

CHAPTER 1:
THE PROCESS OF CONVERSION

HISTORY OF CONVERSION

Multi-unit dwellings first became popular in high population density areas, such as New York City, because apartment buildings, which are built vertically, take up less space and are better able to house large numbers of people. These first apartment buildings were rental properties, owned by a landlord, who rented each unit for a profit.

A number of factors led to conversion of these rental properties into co-op or condominium buildings. Rent control and stabilization laws discouraged investment in rental housing because it limited the rents that the landlord could charge, leading to deterioration of the housing due to lack of sufficient funds for proper upkeep of the property. These laws caused a financial hardship on landlords who started losing money on their investment in the rental property after inflation caused maintenance costs to skyrocket while rents remained low. The landlord was stuck with a money-losing investment because nobody wanted to buy a building with a negative cash flow.

Instead of trying to sell the entire rental property, landlords began to convert their rental buildings into co-op or condominium properties, and were able to make money by selling the individual units. Tenants of the property were given information in the form of an offering plan regarding their right to purchase their unit at an "insider" price. If a tenant was not interested in purchasing their unit, they were permitted to remain a rental tenant and continue to pay the legal rent pursuant to the rent control or stabilization law, whichever applied to the property.

This chapter discusses the general process of converting a multi-unit rental property into a cooperative or condominium property. Because there may be variations in this process among the states, the reader is advised to check the law of his or her own jurisdiction for specific information.

PRELIMINARY OFFERING PLAN

Before an owner/sponsor may convert a rental property, they must present an offering plan to each tenant and to the designated governmental authority, e.g., the State Attorney General. The preliminary offering plan is merely a prospectus of the proposed conversion. The preliminary offering plan is referred to as a "red herring" because of the bold red lettering on the cover of the plan.

The information contained in the preliminary offering plan is subject to review and may be supplemented or changed as determined by the Attorney General. The owner/sponsor may also change the terms of the offering plan. Until the review is completed, and the final version of the plan is accepted for filing, no sales or advertisements are permitted.

In some states, such as New York, interests in a cooperative, condominium or homeowners' association may not be sold, or even offered for sale, until an offering plan—disclosing all the material facts and complying with all of the laws—has been submitted to, and accepted for filing by the state's Attorney General.

Before accepting the plan for filing, the Attorney General's office reviews the preliminary offering plan and supporting documents submitted by the owner/sponsor to determine whether they have complied with tenant protection laws and whether the plan appears to disclose all of the information required by all applicable laws and regulations.

By accepting the plan for filing, the Attorney General is merely indicating whether the owner/sponsor appears to have complied with the law. Responsibility for full compliance lies with the owner/sponsor. Acceptance does not mean the Attorney General has approved the financial terms, the price, the description of the building's condition or any other aspect of the plan.

INDEPENDENT EVALUATION

While the offering plan is being reviewed, the tenants should make their own independent evaluation of the offering plan. Outside professionals, such as attorneys and engineers, can be hired in order to evaluate the plan and assess the condition of the building. If it turns out that there is a conflict between the information gathered through the independent evaluation, and the information contained in the offering plan, this should be brought to the attention of the Attorney General for further investigation.

ACCEPTANCE OF THE PRELIMINARY OFFERING PLAN

Once the Attorney General's office has finished their review and determines that there has been adequate disclosure, the offering plan is accepted for filing. The owner/sponsor may choose between two methods to convert the building: (a) an eviction plan; and (b) a non-eviction plan. An eviction plan can subsequently be changed to a non-eviction plan if the circumstances dictate, however, a non-eviction plan cannot be changed to an eviction plan.

Eviction Plan

In general, under an eviction plan, a non-purchasing tenant may be evicted from an apartment after a certain period of time. In order for an eviction plan to be in effect, 51% of the tenants in occupancy must sign written purchase agreements on the date the offering plan is accepted for filing. If the owner/sponsor does not obtain the required percentage of purchase agreements within a specified time period following the acceptance date, the conversion plan is considered abandoned, and no new conversion plan may be submitted for at least one year.

Under an eviction plan, non-purchasing tenants may not be evicted for a minimum number of years from the date the eviction plan is declared effective, and eligible senior citizen and disabled tenants may not be evicted at any time, unless they breach their leases. Rent-stabilized tenants whose leases expire less than the minimum number of years after the date the plan is declared effective are entitled to renewals, subject to rent increases authorized by the Rent Stabilization Law, extending the lease to the end of the designated time period. Rent-stabilized tenants whose leases already extend beyond this time period may not be evicted until their leases expire.

During this time period, the tenants must be provided all of the services and facilities required by law without discrimination between purchasing and non-purchasing tenants. In addition, apartments subject to government regulation, such as rent control, continue to be covered by those laws until the tenant moves out or until government regulation of the apartment ends, and tenants that occupy apartments that are not subject to government regulation cannot be charged unconscionable rents. Nevertheless, non-purchasing tenants may be subject to eviction for nonpayment of rent, illegal use or occupancy of the premises, or any breach by the tenant of obligations under the rental agreement.

Non-Eviction Plan

Under a non-eviction plan, non-purchasing tenants may not be evicted for failure to buy their apartments and may continue to occupy them as rental tenants.

Rights of Senior Citizens during Conversion

Senior citizens are usually protected against eviction if they choose not to purchase their apartments. However, to be eligible for this protection, a senior citizen, or his or her spouse, must be renting an apartment in a jurisdiction that has adopted a law offering such protection, and must have reached a certain age—e.g., 62—on the date the plan is accepted for filing by the Attorney General.

In those jurisdictions, the senior citizen must complete a special exemption form and submit it to the owner/sponsor within a certain time period after receiving the final offering plan. Nevertheless, eligible senior citizens have the right to subsequently change their minds and become purchasers, and can purchase at the price offered to other tenants in the building at the time they inform the owner/sponsor of their decision to buy.

As a person exempt from eviction, a senior citizen may stay in the apartment after the building is converted, as long as rent is paid and other obligations are met. The apartment may be sold, in which case the buyer becomes the senior citizen's new landlord, and all of the responsibilities of the previous landlord to maintain the property become the responsibility of the new owner. If the apartment was covered by rent control, rent stabilization before conversion, that law continues to apply after conversion.

Rights of Disabled Persons During Conversion

To be eligible for protection against eviction, a disabled person must satisfy all four of the following conditions as of the date the offering plan is accepted for filing:

1. The tenant or spouse must have an impairment which results from anatomical, physiological or psychological conditions, other than addiction to alcohol, gambling or any controlled substance, which is demonstrable by medically acceptable clinical and laboratory diagnostic techniques; and

2. The impairment must be expected to be permanent; and

3. The impairment must prevent the tenant from engaging in any substantial gainful employment; and

4. The tenant or spouse must elect not to purchase the apartment by

completing a special form distributed by the owner/sponsor in the final offering plan. The completed form must be given to the owner/sponsor within a specified number of days from the date the accepted plan was presented to the tenants.

Tenants who first become disabled after the plan is accepted for filing may still qualify as eligible disabled persons, subject to certain legal conditions. They must complete the appropriate forms within a specified number of days following the onset of the disability.

As with senior citizens, eligible disabled persons may stay in the apartment after the building is converted, as long as rent is paid and other obligations are met. The apartment may be sold, in which case the buyer becomes the senior citizen's new landlord, and all of the responsibilities of the previous landlord to maintain the property become the responsibility of the new owner. If the apartment was covered by rent control, or rent stabilization before conversion, that law continues to apply after conversion.

The owner/sponsor can dispute the eligibility of a senior citizen or disabled person by informing the Attorney General that he or she disputes the eligibility of a person claiming senior citizen or disabled status. After reviewing all of the relevant documentation, the Attorney General will issue a determination as to the eligibility of the individual in question.

THE FINAL OFFERING PLAN

The final offering plan is referred to as the "black book" because the bold red lettering contained on the preliminary offering plan (the "red herring") is replaced with black lettering indicating the date the final plan was accepted for filing. The final offering plan constitutes the owner/sponsor's offer to sell co-op or condo units on the terms and conditions set forth in the plan. Each tenant receives a copy of the final offering plan.

Conversion is not automatic even if the plan has been accepted. For example, a specified number of apartments must be purchased before the plan can be declared effective and the building actually converted. The owner/sponsor may also choose to abandon the offering plan and continue to operate the building as a rental property.

In general, tenants have the exclusive right to buy their apartments, or the corresponding shares of stock, for a certain period of time after the final offering plan is presented to them. During this time period, the tenant's apartment may not be shown to a prospective buyer unless the tenant has, in writing, waived the right to purchase.

For an additional time period after the exclusive purchase period has expired, tenants facing eviction may still purchase their apartments, but at this time they must purchase on the same terms as non-tenants. If an occupied apartment is sold to an outside purchaser during this time period, the owner/sponsor must notify the tenant who must match the terms of the contract and purchase the apartment within a specified number of days. Tenants of apartments covered by the government regulation, e.g., rental control, also have the right to match an outside offer for purchase of their apartments.

Apartments unsold at the time a plan is declared effective remain the property of the owner/sponsor, who may sell them for whatever the market will bear. Because the law specifies that the conversion plan may only be declared effective after a specified percentage of the tenants of occupied apartments have agreed to purchase, the owner of a building who contemplates submitting a plan for its conversion to co-op or condo ownership might have some incentive to discourage renting vacant apartments. In some jurisdictions this practice, called "warehousing", is restricted; a conversion plan may be rejected by the Attorney General if he finds that excessive warehousing has occurred.

Specifically, if the Attorney General determines that during the five months immediately preceding submission of the preliminary offering plan, the number of vacant apartments has exceeded a specified percentage of the total number of rental units in the building, and if that rate is more than double the "normal" average vacancy rate for the previous calendar years, the plan will not be accepted for filing.

Conversion laws generally prohibit any person from interrupting, discontinuing or interfering with any essential service which substantially disturbs the comfort or peace and quiet of any tenant who uses or occupies an apartment. The tenant, or the Attorney General, may take legal action to stop harassment.

OBTAINING LEGAL REPRESENTATION

The conversion of a rental apartment building to a cooperative or condominium is a technical and complex process. Experience has shown that a tenant, whose building is being converted to a co-op or condo may want to consult a lawyer to ensure that his/her rights are being protected. An attorney familiar with the conversion process will be able to explain it completely, and may be retained to represent the tenants in their negotiations with the building owner.

If you are considering buying a condo, or buying shares in a cooperative corporation, you should also consult a lawyer and an accountant, just as you would if you were buying a house. An accountant will aid you in understanding the financial statements contained in the offering plan you receive before purchasing. This purchase may be the most important financial transaction of your life, and you should have all the facts needed to make an intelligent and well-informed decision.

CHAPTER 2:
WHAT IS A CO-OP?

COOPERATIVE OWNERSHIP

Co-op is a shortened version of the word cooperative. Cooperative ownership refers to the ownership of an entire multi-unit development by the tenants as a whole. When you own a co-op, you own personal property—i.e., you own shares of stock in the corporation that owns the real estate. You do not own the actual unit you are living in, whether it is a townhouse in a community setting, or an apartment in a multi-unit building. Because cooperative properties involve ownership of shares of stock in a corporation, co-ops are governed by state statutes.

Each unit is allocated a certain number of shares based on such factors as the location and size of each unit, and the number of rooms. The allocation of shares must be fair and reasonable. For example, the owner of a 2-bedroom unit would own more shares in the corporation than the owner of a studio apartment.

Instead of rent, the co-op owner pays what is known as a maintenance fee, which usually includes the real estate taxes, the cost of maintaining the property, and a monthly assessment. If there is an underlying mortgage, the co-op owner must also pay his or her proportionate share of the loan. Maintenance fees are discussed more fully below.

If you are interested in building equity in the co-op you purchase, you must familiarize yourself with the different types of co-ops on the market, as set forth below.

1. Market Rate Cooperative—If you purchase a market rate cooperative, you can buy or sell your shares at the market price, similar to a condo or single family home.

2. Limited Equity Cooperative—If you purchase a limited equity cooperative, the bylaws generally restrict the amount you can profit

from the sale of your shares in the corporation. This makes housing more affordable and allows the owner to benefit from below-market interest rate loans.

3. Zero Equity Cooperatives—If you purchase a zero equity cooperative, also referred to as a "leasing cooperative," you cannot build equity because the corporation leases the property from a third party. The corporation cannot build equity in property it does not own. However, the corporation can always convert a zero equity cooperative into a market rate or limited equity cooperative if it decides to purchase the property.

PROPRIETARY LEASE

In return for purchasing stock in the corporation, you are given a long-term renewable proprietary lease entitling you to occupy the unit. Your proprietary lease sets forth your rights and obligations as a co-op owner, and contains restrictions which you must follow concerning use and occupancy of your unit.

For example, the lease may restrict how many people can occupy the unit, and whether pets are allowed. The lease may also limit the amount of financing you can obtain when you use your shares in the corporation as collateral. Your lease may prohibit you from subletting your unit, or limit the amount of time you are allowed to sublet.

Your lease may also prohibit you from making any major renovations that may affect the underlying structure of the property, such as taking out a wall. You are generally required to obtain board approval and submit your plans to the board. The co-op board cannot unreasonably reject your renovation plans.

COOPERATIVE MAINTENANCE FEES

The cooperative corporation is required to pay property taxes, insurance premiums, heating costs, and operating expenses, including salaries for corporation employees. The cooperative corporation may also be required to make payments on any underlying mortgages on the property. The underlying mortgage may have existed from the time the cooperative purchased the property, or for funds borrowed to make repairs and capital improvements.

These expenses are passed on to the co-op owners who occupy the co-op units, based on the number of shares allocated to the particular unit. Each co-op owner is required to pay their portion of the corporation's expenses—known as the maintenance fee—on a monthly basis. If you fail to pay your required fees, you can be evicted.

Co-op maintenance fees are often higher than the common charges paid by condo owners, however, the co-op fee includes many items not covered by common charges, such as the co-op owner's share of property taxes, and contribution to any underlying mortgage on the cooperative property.

The maintenance fee may also include insurance premiums, and reserve funds for repairs, utilities, etc. In addition, if the property has recreational facilities, such as a pool and tennis courts, etc., your maintenance fee will be higher. Although maintenance fees tend to be stable, they may go up if there is an increase in property taxes, or if the corporation needs to apply for additional financing, e.g., if major repairs are needed or there is an rise in operating expenses.

The maintenance fee, along with the loan the purchaser obtained to finance the shares in the corporation, makes up the co-op owner's total monthly costs for occupying the unit.

THE BOARD OF DIRECTORS

The cooperative corporation is managed by a board of directors. Members of the board are elected by the co-op owners, and usually live within the cooperative property. As a co-op owner, you also have the right to remove board members if you are dissatisfied with their service. The board's powers and responsibilities are detailed in the corporation's bylaws, a copy of which must be included in the offering plan. Co-op owners also have the right to amend the bylaws.

The rights and obligations of individual co-op owners are also explained in the bylaws of the corporation, as well as in the proprietary lease, the articles of incorporation, subscription agreement, and house rules. All co-op owners are entitled to copies of these documents. You can request them from your co-op's corporate office or from your co-op's managing agent.

The board makes the rules that govern the day-to-day operations of the cooperative. When you purchase shares in a co-op, you are required to sign an agreement stating that you will abide by these rules. For example, board rules may require co-op owners to maintain their properties in a certain manner, e.g., mow the grass regularly, replace doors or windows, etc. You must comply or arguably you would be in violation of the rules and subject to the penalties set forth in those rules. Insofar as you do not hold title to your individual unit when you own shares in a co-op, you can be evicted if you violate the co-op rules and regulations.

Many cooperative corporations hire managing agents to operate the property if permitted under the co-op's established bylaws. The managing agent's responsibilities include collecting maintenance fees from the co-op owners, and supervising employees of the corporation. The managing agent receives a fee from the corporation for performing these services.

RESTRICTIONS ON SALES

Co-op rules may place restrictions upon the sale of your unit, requiring prior approval from the board. The board makes decisions on who can purchase your shares of the corporation and move into your unit. The prospective buyer is usually required to complete a formal application, undergo a credit check, and attend an interview with the board.

The board approval process is perhaps the most significant difference between co-ops and condos. Traditionally, the required board interview with the prospective buyer was viewed as a method of keeping undesirable people out of the property. However, the stated reasoning behind the interview is to educate the intended purchaser about the responsibilities of cooperative ownership. Another reason for the board interview is to review the buyer's application packet, which typically includes detailed financial information and letters of reference.

The board can generally refuse a prospective buyer for any reason it deems appropriate. For example, based on your income, if the board determines that you are unable to pay the monthly ownership fees, your application may be rejected on financial grounds. In addition, if you do not intend to be an owner-occupant but plan to sublet the property, you can be turned down. Further, if the board determines that there are too many people in your family based on the size of the unit you intend to occupy, your application may be denied.

Discrimination Prohibited

Although the board has broad power to reject prospective co-op owners, it cannot do so on a discriminatory basis. For example, you cannot be turned down based on your race, nationality, religion, or because you have a disability. This would violate federal law. In addition, there are state laws which may provide even greater protection against discrimination, e.g., based on sexual orientation. The reader is advised to check the law of his or her jurisdiction.

Your rights and remedies if you suspect you are a victim of housing discrimination is set forth in Chapter 6 of this almanac.

ADVANTAGES OF CO-OP OWNERSHIP

Despite the restrictions placed on co-op owners, there are advantages to buying a co-op.

Affordability

The co-op is usually more affordable than a condo or single family home. Generally, there is a lower down payment required for financing the co-op, and lower closing costs because, unlike a condo, there is no mortgage recording tax, title insurance or tax escrow involved in financing a co-op. In addition, the monthly maintenance fee is usually stable unless there is an unexpected rise in real estate taxes or operating costs, which are included in your maintenance fee.

Tax Deductions

Co-op owners have the same potential tax benefits as owners of condos or single family homes. The taxes and interest on the underlying building mortgage you pay to the corporation as part of the monthly maintenance fee are tax deductible. In addition, the interest—but not the principal—that you pay on your loan to finance the purchase of the shares is also deductible. The deduction can be substantial.

You must claim your deduction on Schedule A of your 1040 federal income tax return. You must itemize your deductions on your tax return in order to benefit. Section 216 is the section of the Internal Revenue Code that allows the pass-through of mortgage interest and real property tax deductions from the cooperative housing corporation to the co-op owners.

Section 216 of the Internal Revenue Code is set forth at Appendix 1.

In addition to the economic benefits co-op ownership offers, you do are not responsible for making major repairs or for the upkeep of the property. The board is generally responsible for making sure the property is adequately maintained.

CHAPTER 3:
WHAT IS A CONDO?

CONDOMINIUM OWNERSHIP

Condo is a shortened version of the word condominium. The condominium is a statutorily created form of ownership of real estate. When you own a condominium, you own real property—i.e., you own the actual unit in which you live. You have a deed to your property, whether it is an individual apartment in a building or a townhouse in a community setting. Thus, unlike a co-op owner, you cannot be evicted from your condo.

Although owning a condo is similar to home ownership in that you have a deed and the condo can be bought or sold, you only exercise ownership over the interior of your dwelling. Each individual owner owns an undivided joint ownership interest in the common areas of the real estate for which they pay a common charge for the maintenance of those areas. Common areas generally include the land on which the building is located, the lobby, public halls, driveways, access roads and parking areas. The electrical, mechanical, heating and air conditioning systems that service the building are also considered common elements.

Because condominiums are not owned by corporations, the way co-ops are owned, they are not governed by state corporation laws. Instead, each state has enacted its own law concerning the organization and operation of condominiums. If the law sets forth certain requirements, the condominium association must adhere to them.

Although these laws vary in their complexity, they generally require the condominium to file a declaration and bylaws, and to detail the rights and responsibilities of the association. The condominium declaration describes the individual units and the common areas, and sets forth any restrictions on the use or occupancy of the units.

As an example of state condominium law, New York's Condominium Act is set forth at Appendix 2.

CONDOMINIUM COMMON CHARGES

One of the requirements of condominium ownership is the payment of monthly expenses to cover general repairs and maintenance to the common areas of the property, and a proportionate share of the fuel costs, employee salaries, and other expenses of operation. These costs are known as common charges. Also included in the common charges is a contribution to the condominium association's cash reserve for future repairs or other needs.

In general, all exterior maintenance and repairs are the responsibility of the condominium association. These expenses are passed through to the condo owners as part of the monthly common charges or through a special assessment. A special assessment is a one time expense charged to all condo owners on a pro rata basis. However, special assessments are usually subject to a vote by either the condominium association or by all of the condo owners.

Unlike the co-op maintenance fee, real estate taxes are not included in the condominium common charge. The condo owner pays the property taxes directly to the taxing authority. You will receive a tax bill each year just like you would if you owned a house. The tax bill includes the value of your unit and undivided share of the land and common facilities.

CONDOMINIUM ASSOCIATION

The condominium is governed by a board of managers elected by the condo owners, generally referred to as the condominium association. The association's authority to operate the property is explained in detail in the condominium declaration and bylaws. Like the co-op board, the association makes the rules that govern the day-to-day operations of the condominium, which the condo owners must follow.

In general, the condominium association is responsible for the exterior upkeep of the property, and may raise or lower assessments and impose special assessments to cover specific repairs or improvements. The association may also insist that owners obey the declaration and bylaws of the condominium.

When a condo owner ignores the rules, the association can assess fines against the owner. The fines, if substantial, can be filed as a lien against the owner's property, and the property can be foreclosed upon in order for the association to collect the fines.

A sample condominium fine policy is set forth at Appendix 3.

If there is a certain practice that the association wants the owner to stop doing—such as posting advertisements—the association can sue the owner in court and obtain an injunction to stop the owner from continuing the objectionable practice. If the owner continues despite the court order, he or she can be found in contempt.

In any event, if the association does decide to take the owner to court, it must do so immediately. If the association lets certain practices continue without taking immediate action, it may lose its right to object for failure to enforce the rule or regulation.

CONDOMINIUM DOCUMENTS

Prospective condo buyers are entitled to receive a detailed description of all material financial, legal and engineering aspects of the property that the buyer wants to purchase. This group of documents is referred to as the "offering plan." The offering plan is intended to satisfy the legal requirements of summarizing and disclosing important information concerning the condo before the buyer is legally committed to purchase it.

In some states, such as New York, the buyer is given a certain period of time—e.g., seven days—to review the offering plan before the buyer may be legally obligated to purchase the property. This is so even if there is already a signed contract in place between the seller and buyer.

The offering plan must contain a description of the physical aspects of the property, including the equipment and fixtures, and a projection of the buyer's future financial obligations, including the buyer's estimated closing costs, real estate taxes, and common charges. The offering plan must also summarize and set out completely the condominium documents, including the declaration of condominium, the bylaws, and any other governing documents for the condominium.

The Condominium Declaration

The condominium declaration is the legal document recorded in the land records office of the jurisdiction in which the property is located. It is the document that creates the condominium. The declaration describes with specificity the property, and many of the important details, including the boundaries of the units; the things that will make up the common elements, including limited common elements; a determination of the unit owner's percentage interest in the common elements; the purposes and restrictions on the use of the property; provisions for easements and provisions concerning assessments and liens against the units; and the liability of the unit owner for payment of the common expenses.

The Bylaws

The bylaws are the constitution of the condominium association. The bylaws contain the rules for self-government of the association, and cover such matters as requirements for meetings, voting, the manner in which the budget should be prepared, the determination and handling of assessments, including special assessments and the filing of assessment liens, the nature of insurance coverage, and restrictions on the use of the units and the common areas.

Declaration of Covenants, Conditions and Restrictions

Every condominium is required to file a declaration of covenants, conditions and restrictions. The declaration provide rules and procedures for conducting the affairs of the condominium, and define the rights and obligations of unit owners. For example, if the condominium has restrictions on pets, children, re-sale and leasing, those restrictions would be included in the declaration.

RIGHTS AND OBLIGATIONS OF CONDO OWNERS

The prospective purchaser generally has a three-day right of rescission during which they are allowed by law to cancel the condominium purchase contract. Thus, as soon as you have received all of the condominium documents, you should read them carefully to decide whether you will be able to comply with the obligations and restrictions imposed on condo owners. Such obligations and restrictions may include:

1. The monthly common charges and the likelihood that they will increase in the future.

2. Special assessments which may be imposed.

3. Restrictions on your right to sell, lease, or mortgage your condo.

4. Restrictions on the age of children who may use the pool, beach or other recreational facilities.

5. Restrictions on pets.

6. Restrictions on parking vehicles or boats other than regular passenger automobiles.

7. Restrictions on types of floor-covering materials, drapes or window hangings.

8. Restrictions on screening open balconies.

9. Your obligations to maintain windows, screens, air conditioners, plumbing, etc.

10. Any mandatory club memberships or recreation facility leases in connection with the condominium.

11. Limitations on the use of recreational facilities.

Each condo owner is entitled to vote on matters of interest based upon their ownership percentage of the common areas of the condominium.

Although day-to-day maintenance of the property is the responsibility of the condominium association, interior maintenance and repairs of the condo unit are the responsibility of the individual owner. Additionally, each condominium owner pays real estate taxes, separately assessed against each unit, and the cost of any mortgage obtained to finance the original purchase.

Condo owners are allowed to decorate the interior of their property, however, any major renovations are governed by the rules and regulations of the condo association. Generally, any renovations that would result in a structural, mechanical or electrical change, would require prior approval.

Unlike the co-op board, the condominium association cannot prevent you from selling your condo to whomever you choose. The only right a condo association may have in this regard is the right of first refusal—i.e., the right to buy your unit at the same terms as the prospective buyer. In practice, however, condo associations rarely exercise this right.

ADVANTAGES TO CONDO OWNERSHIP

Affordability

In general, the same square footage will cost less in a condo setting than it will in a single family home or townhouse, due mainly to land cost—i.e., you can build many more condos than you can single family homes on the same amount of land.

Tax Deductions

Condo owners have the same potential tax benefits as homeowners. The property taxes that are paid directly to the taxing authority by the condo owner are tax deductible. In addition, the interest—but not the principal—that you pay on your mortgage loan is tax deductible. The deduction from taxable income can be substantial.

CHAPTER 4:
PURCHASING A CO-OP OR CONDO

PREPARATION

Because purchasing a co-op, condo or home is an investment, you must be able to put in the time and money necessary to maintain your investment. Before you decide to buy purchase, you should consider whether the timing is right for you.

For example, you will need the time and energy to maintain the property, e.g., make necessary repairs, mow the lawn, etc. In addition, it is important that you have a steady, reliable source of income. Regular employment and income is important so that you can qualify for a financing, and so you do not default on your loans and lose your investment. You must have enough income to cover all of your outstanding debts, the loan payments, and costs related to your property, such as real estate taxes and insurance. In addition, you must have saved enough money for the downpayment and closing costs.

Before you begin searching for a place to live, it is also helpful to establish a list of criteria which contains both the essential qualities and the non-essential qualities you are looking for in your new home. If you have not yet decided whether you want to purchase a co-op or condominium, you should understand the basic difference between the two forms of ownership.

A comparison chart demonstrating the differences between co-op and condo ownership is set forth at Appendix 4.

Don't waste time looking at housing that doesn't meet your minimum requirements, however, don't pass up suitable housing that may not meet all of your criteria. It is unlikely that any one co-op or condo will meet your every need and every wish, both essential and non-essential.

A U.S. Housing and Urban Development (HUD) checklist provided for determining essential and non-essential housing criteria is set forth at Appendix 5, and a HUD checklist designed to assist the buyer in evaluating prospective housing is set forth at Appendix 6.

It is important to find out how many units exist in the complex, and how many are occupied. It is also important to find out whether the monthly assessments are being collected in a timely manner, and if there is a sufficient reserve of funds to meet any unexpected repairs or other expenses. This will give you an idea of the financial stability of the development.

The financial condition of the cooperative corporation or condominium is very important and merits a close examination. There should be an annual financial budget which sets forth both income and expenses, as well as the present financial condition, including the cash reserves on hand. The more solvent the development, the more protected the owners. If there is a lack of cash reserves and a major repair becomes necessary, the development will be looking to you, the owner, for the necessary funds. This would be accomplished by charging a special assessment to all of the co-op/condo owners.

You should also clarify the amount of the monthly maintenance fee or common charge, and determine what items are included in the monthly assessment. Although all of the restrictions will be contained in the co-op or condo documents, you should find out up front whether there are any restrictions that would definitely preclude you from purchasing the unit, such as restrictions on pets, subleases, etc. If these are non-negotiable restrictions, it doesn't make sense to go forward with negotiations as the seller will not be able to unilaterally dispense with those restrictions on your behalf.

When you visit the property, do not limit yourself to the particular unit you are interested in purchasing. You should also take time to walk through the common areas, check out the pool, recreational facilities, and other amenities. Are the common areas kept clean? Is the pool well-maintained? Visit the development at different times of the day and week.

Speak with some of your prospective neighbors to get a feel for the community and the satisfaction or dissatisfaction of the residents. You may be able to find out whether there is an open line of communication between the co-op/condo owners and the co-op board/condominium association. You may also discover whether there are any pending lawsuits against the development, and the claims involved in those lawsuits. It is advisable to prepare a list of questions covering all of the above issues before visiting the co-op/condominium complex.

A list of suggested questions is set forth at Appendix 7.

LEGAL REPRESENTATION

If you find a co-op or condominium unit you are considering purchasing, it is advisable that you retain an attorney who is familiar with the co-op/condo law before purchasing. Do not sign the purchase contract without first consulting your attorney.

Your attorney will review the purchase contract, declaration, bylaws, and any other governing documents to make sure they comply with state law, and do not contain any hidden problems. Your attorney will explain all of your rights and responsibilities as a co-op or condo owner. You need to know what restrictions apply, particularly with a co-op, and decide whether they are so unduly burdensome that it is not worth the investment.

Example: You are interested in a unit, however, the kitchen/dining area is very small. You would like to knock out a wall in order to expand the area. You must find out if there are any architectural restrictions which would prohibit you from knocking out the wall. If so, will you be able to obtain a variance—i.e., permission to remove the wall despite the restriction? If not, do you still want the unit despite the small kitchen/dining area?

There is usually a certain period of time within which you can rescind the contract if you change your mind. The time period varies, and may depend on whether you are purchasing the unit from a developer or a private owner.

GOING TO CONTRACT

Once you have decided to purchase a particular co-op or condo unit, you must generally submit a verbal offer through your real estate agent. If your offer is accepted, the seller's attorney will draw up a contract and send it to your attorney, who will review the terms of the contract with you. If you are satisfied with the terms of the contract, you will sign it and submit it to the seller with the required down payment—usually 10-20% of the purchase price. The down payment is held in escrow until the closing.

The seller will sign the contract and return it to your attorney. You do not have a contract until the seller signs the contract. Although most sellers will not continue to show the property once there has been an accepted offer, the seller is not bound to sell the property to you until the contact is signed. Therefore, if you are really interested in the property, it is advisable for your attorney to have the contract fully executed as soon as possible.

APPLICATION AND INTERVIEW PROCESS

If your purchase requires co-op board or condo association approval, you will need to complete the application and submit any requested supporting documentation, such as your net worth statement. After your application has been reviewed, a personal interview will be scheduled. Once you receive approval, and your financing is in place, you will be able to finalize the purchase at the real estate closing.

PRE-CLOSING INSPECTION

Shortly before the closing, you will be given the opportunity to examine the house in a "final walk-through." Generally, the unit is supposed to be turned over in "broom-swept" condition. At this time, the house is usually empty, so you are able to take a close look at floors, walls and ceilings, and any requested repairs. If there are any problems discovered during the walk-through, they should be taken care of prior to closing.

THE REAL ESTATE CLOSING

The real estate closing may be held at the office of the building management company, or at the office of one of the attorneys. The persons attending the closing usually include a representative from building management, the purchaser and the purchaser's attorney, the seller and the seller's attorney, the lender's attorney, and the real estate agent. There may also be a title company representative if the purchase involves a condominium. You will receive the keys to your unit at the closing.

CHAPTER 5:
FINANCING

IN GENERAL

Once the contract is signed, you must apply for a loan. Prior to applying for financing, it is prudent to make sure all of your finances are in order, and gather all of the documents that may be required by the lender. It is also a good idea to pay off any debts you can manage to eliminate.

A formula is used by many lenders in determining whether a prospective buyer has sufficient funds to afford the property they are purchasing. For example, if you are buying a co-op, your annual housing expenses should not exceed 25 to 30 percent of your gross income, and your total debt should not exceed 35 to 40 percent.

CHECK YOUR CREDIT REPORTS

You should review your credit reports from each of the three credit reporting agencies to make sure they are accurate and up-to-date. If not, you should have any incorrect information removed from your credit report before you apply for financing. Contact information for the three major credit reporting agencies is as follows:

EQUIFAX
P.O. Box 740241
Atlanta, GA 30374
Phone: (800) 685-1111
Website: www.equifax.com

EXPERIAN
National Consumer Assistance Center
P.O. Box 2002
Allen, TX 75013
Phone: (888) EXPERIAN
Website: www.experian.com/consumer/

TRANS UNION LLC
Consumer Disclosure Center
P.O. Box 1000
Chester, PA 19022
Phone: (800) 888-4213
Website: www.transunion.com

GATHER DOCUMENTS

You can speed up the loan process by providing the lender with all of the necessary financial documents as quickly as possible. Following are some of the documents you should gather in anticipation of applying for financing:

1. Reference letters from both personal friends and business associates.

2. Employment verification.

3. Proof of income, including tax returns and W-2 forms covering at least the two prior years, and any award letters from social security, pension funds, etc.

4. Bank account verification and statements.

5. Brokerage statements.

6. Net Worth Statement.

7. Mortgage loan application and commitment letter.

8. Authorization for credit check.

9. A certificate of insurance showing how much insurance has been purchased to cover damages to the common areas and any general insurance for your unit

10. A certificate of title that shows clear title to your unit.

11. Copies of the bylaws and the Covenants, Conditions and Restrictions (CC&Rs).

FINANCING A CONDO VS. FINANCING A CO-OP

Due to the two vastly different types of ownership involved, financing a co-op is quite different from financing a condominium, as set forth below.

Condo Financing

Although a prospective buyer may purchase a condo on an all cash basis, it is more likely that the buyer will finance a large part of the purchase price through a real estate lender. Financing a condo is much like financing a single family home. You must apply for a mortgage, and the lender will be granted a lien on the condominium unit. Real estate taxes and mortgage interest are tax-deductible.

A mortgage loan may be obtained from a bank, a savings and loan, a credit union, a private mortgage company, or from various state government lenders. There are a wide variety of condominium loans available in the marketplace, including 100% financing. These favor buyers with good credit and earning potential, but little money to put down.

Different lenders can offer quite different interest rates and loan fees so it is wise to shop around. The reader is advised to check the real estate or business sections in the newspaper for information on current interest rates, and to undertake some comparative shopping. One should call several lenders for rates and terms based on the type of mortgage sought. Be aware that the lower the interest, the smaller the monthly payment.

It is also important to ask each lender for a complete list of closing costs and inquire as to which costs will be refunded to you if the loan application is not approved.

The Mortgage Payment

A mortgage payment represents interest and principal. In the early years of a mortgage loan, the majority of the payment is credited towards interest. The remaining portion of the payment, and any payment you make above the minimum payment, is credited towards principal. In the later years of a mortgage loan, the majority of the payment is credited towards principal, and the smaller portion goes towards interest. When you have a fixed rate mortgage loan, your monthly payment remains the same throughout the loan. This makes it easier to plan for the future.

Building Equity

If you own a condo, you are building equity when you make your monthly mortgage payment. Equity generally represents the difference between the current market value of your condo, and the amount of the outstanding mortgage loan. Another financial advantage to owning a condo is the possibility its value will go up through the years, building more equity in your investment.

Tax Deductions

The mortgage interest on your loan is deductible from your federal income tax. Some states also allow the deduction. This results in a significant tax savings, particularly in the early years when the interest payments are highest.

More detailed information on obtaining a mortgage can be found in this author's legal almanac entitled Buying and Selling Your Home, published by Oceana Publishing Company.

Co-op Financing

If you are financing a co-op, you would apply for a personal loan to finance your purchase of the shares allocated to the co-op unit. You pledge your shares of stock and proprietary lease as security for the loan. The lender's lien is filed against your shares in the corporation, not the co-op unit. This type of financing is generally referred to as a "share loan," not a mortgage.

The co-op board establishes the amount of financing you are allowed to apply for—usually between 50 and 75 percent. The interest on the loan is tax deductible. Your payments on the share loan, along with your monthly maintenance fee, constitute your total carrying charges for the co-op unit. Some lenders permit the purchaser to roll the balance of the purchaser's pro rata share of the cooperative's underlying mortgage into their primary share loan.

Assessing the Risk

Not all lenders will finance a co-op. Lenders are more cautious when it comes to making loans involving co-ops. There is more risk inherent in buying a co-op as opposed to buying a condo because you are not buying your individual unit, you are buying shares in a corporation. The lender most consider the stability of the corporation. If the corporation is having financial problems, shareholders could lose their shares in the corporation, and any money they invested.

One red flag that a lender looks for is whether there is a disproportionate number of unoccupied units in the cooperative property. If so, the corporation may not receive enough income to maintain the property and pay the underlying mortgage, particularly if there is a large balloon payment due.

Therefore, it is important to review the cooperative corporation's financial statements. The financial statements should contain a summary of the corporation's assets and liabilities, including various potential liabilities. Because co-op owners share the operating costs and liabilities of the cooperative corporation, it is most important for a buyer to have the information from the financial statements from at least the two most recent fiscal years of operation before making a purchase decision.

Following are some key questions to ask when reviewing the financial statements of the corporation:

1. Does the corporation have working capital of at least 3-4 months of regular operating expenses?

2. Is the corporation collecting more in maintenance charges than it is paying in operating expenses?

3. Are there any pending potential liabilities such as lawsuits that the corporation will be required to pay and in turn require reimbursement from the co-op owners?

4. Does the corporation maintain a reserve for capital replacements of worn out equipment and structures such as elevators, heating, ventilating and air-conditioning equipment, the roof and other exterior portions of the building, plumbing and electrical systems and other upgrades and improvements of the building that are periodically required?

CHAPTER 6:
HOUSING DISCRIMINATION

THE FAIR HOUSING ACT

Many co-ops are selective in approving prospective owners. However, like any other type of housing, co-ops are not allowed to discriminate based on the protected classes listed in the Fair Housing Act (Title VIII of the Civil Rights Act of 1968).

The Fair Housing Act prohibits discrimination in the sale, rental, and financing of dwellings, and in other housing-related transactions, based on race, color, national origin, religion, sex, familial status (including children under the age of 18 living with parents of legal custodians, pregnant women, and people securing custody of children under the age of 18), and handicap (disability).

In response to evidence of continuing housing discrimination, Congress passed the Fair Housing Act Amendments of 1988 to provide for more effective enforcement of fair housing rights through judicial and administrative avenues and to expand the number of protected classes covered under Federal fair housing laws.

In general, discrimination in housing occurs when someone:

1. Refuses to rent to you or sell you housing;

2. Tells you housing is unavailable when in fact it is available;

3. Shows you apartments or homes in certain neighborhoods only;

4. Advertises housing to preferred groups of people only;.

5. Refuses to provide you with information regarding mortgage loans, denies you a mortgage loan, or imposes different terms or conditions on a mortgage loan;

6. Denies you property insurance;

7. Conducts property appraisals in a discriminatory manner;

8. Refuses to make certain modifications or accommodations for persons with a with a mental or physical disability, including persons recovering from alcohol and substance abuse, and HIV/AIDS-related illnesses;

9. Fails to design and construct housing in an accessible manner;

10. Harasses, coerces, intimidates, or interferes with anyone exercising or assisting someone else with their fair housing rights.

11. Advertises or makes any statement that indicates a limitation or preference based on race, color, national origin, religion, sex, familial status, or handicap. This prohibition against discriminatory advertising also applies to single-family and owner-occupied housing that is otherwise exempt from the Fair Housing Act.

Persons that may not discriminate include, but are not limited to:

1. Landlords;

2. Resident managers or assistant resident managers;

3. Apartment maintenance crew or other staff;

4. Property managers;

5. Property owners;

6. Newspapers or other sources of advertisement;

7. Real estate agents;

8. Lenders or other financial institutions;

9. Insurance agents or companies;

10. Appraisers;

11. Builders;

12. Architects; and

13. Any other person who designs, constructs or provides housing.

The text of The Fair Housing Act are set forth at Appendix 8.

CONSUMER COMPLAINTS

If you believe you are the victim of housing discrimination, and that you are being excluded from a neighborhood or particular house, immediately contact the U.S. Department of Housing and Urban Development (HUD). Also, contact HUD if you believe you are being discriminated against on the basis of race, color, religion, sex, nationality, familial status, or disability. HUD's Office of Fair Housing has a hotline for reporting incidents of discrimination: (TEL) 1-800-669-9777/(TTY) 1-800-927-9275.

A Directory of HUD Fair Housing Enforcement Centers is set forth at Appendix 9.

You have one year after an alleged violation to file a complaint with HUD, but you should file it as soon as possible. If you believe you have been the victim of housing discrimination, you can file a fair housing complaint with the Office of Fair Housing and Equal Opportunity at the following address:

> Office of Fair Housing and Equal Opportunity
> Department of Housing and Urban Development
> 451 Seventh St. SW, Room 5204
> Washington, DC 20410-2000
> Telephone: (202) 708-1112 TTY: (202) 708-1455

Your complaint should include the following information:

1. Your name and address.

2. The name and address of the person your complaint is about.

3. The address of the house or apartment you were trying to buy.

4. The date when this incident occurred.

5. A short description of what happened.

HUD will notify you when it receives your complaint. In investigating the complaint, HUD will:

1. Notify the alleged violator of your complaint and permit that person to submit an answer;

2. Investigate your complaint and determine whether there is reasonable cause to believe the Fair Housing Act has been violated; and

3. Notify you if it cannot complete an investigation within 100 days of receiving your complaint.

HUD will try to reach a conciliation agreement with the respondent. A conciliation agreement must protect both you and the public interest. If an agreement is signed, HUD will take no further action on your complaint. However, if HUD has reasonable cause to believe that a conciliation agreement is breached, HUD will recommend that the Attorney General file suit.

If HUD has determined that your State or local agency has the same fair housing powers as HUD, HUD will refer your complaint to that agency for investigation and notify you of the referral. That agency must begin work on your complaint within 30 days or HUD may take it back.

If your case goes to an administrative hearing, HUD attorneys will litigate the case on your behalf. You may intervene in the case and be represented by your own attorney if you wish. An Administrative Law Judge will consider evidence from you and the respondent. If the judge decides that discrimination occurred, the respondent can be ordered to take the following actions:

1. Compensate you for actual damages, including humiliation, pain and suffering;

2. Provide injunctive or other equitable relief, for example, to make the housing available to you;

3. Pay the Federal Government a civil penalty to vindicate the public interest. The maximum penalties are $10,000 for a first violation and $50,000 for a third violation within seven years.

4. Pay reasonable attorney's fees and costs.

If you or the respondent choose to have your case decided in Federal District Court, the Attorney General will file a suit and litigate it on your behalf. The District Court can also order relief, and award actual damages, attorney's fees and costs. In addition, the court can award punitive damages.

You may file suit, at your expense, in Federal District Court or state court within two years of an alleged violation. If you cannot afford an attorney, the Court may appoint one for you. You may bring suit even after filing a complaint, if you have not signed a conciliation agreement and an Administrative Law Judge has not started a hearing. A court may award actual and punitive damages and attorney's fees and costs.

CHAPTER 7:
INSURANCE

IN GENERAL

This chapter discusses the various types of insurance you will need to purchase once you become a co-op or condo owner. It is important to understand what each type of policy covers.

TITLE INSURANCE

Title insurance is an indemnity contract that protects the condominium buyer's interests in the property. Title insurance guarantees that when the buyer purchases the condo, he or she will actually own it free and clear of any third party interests or claims. The primary purpose of title insurance is to eliminate risks and prevent losses caused by defects in title arising out of past events.

If the reported title is incorrect or if there are any other liens and interests in the property that the title company did not report to the buyer, then the title company must indemnify the buyer—i.e., pay for any losses the buyer incurs up to the amount of the title insurance policy.

The Title Search

While the title insurance company assumes the risks of a title problem, the title insurer's basic function is to take steps to protect the buyer's property interest and minimize the risks that the buyer will suffer any loss. This is accomplished by undertaking a title search.

The title search is conducted to make sure the condo being purchased has "clear title"—i.e., there are no claims, liens or encumbrances against the property. The title insurer performs an extensive search of the property's title in the public records. All of the prior interests and rights in the property are identified and examined to determine whether they in any way affect the purchaser's title to the property.

Once satisfied that the title is clear, the title insurer prepares a title insurance policy. At the closing, the purchaser will pay a one-time title insurance premium. Title insurance coverage remains in place for as long as the buyer has an interest in the condo.

Title Insurance and Co-op Apartments

As discussed in Chapter 2 of this almanac, co-op buyers acquire ownership by purchasing shares of stock issued by the cooperative corporation. In return, the buyer receives a proprietary lease for the unit. The cooperative corporation actually owns the building and the individual units. Stock ownership is not considered a legal interest in real estate. Rather, it is considered personal property and not the acquisition of real estate.

Therefore, title insurance is not provided for a co-op purchase. A title company will, however, conduct a search of liens that exist against the personal property of the seller. The real estate records are not searched unless the buyer has some concerns about the cooperative corporation itself.

LIABILITY INSURANCE

Co-op and condominium complexes generally maintain liability insurance in case someone is injured in the common areas of the property. Nevertheless, it is prudent to purchase your own personal liability insurance policy in case you are somehow brought into such a lawsuit as a named defendant. Even if you are not legally liable, there is nothing to prevent the injured person from suing you.

Although you may eventually prevail in the lawsuit, you must have liability insurance to cover the attorney fees and costs which are certain to accumulate while you defend yourself. The insurance carrier is obligated to retain an attorney on your behalf, which will give you some peace of mind while the lawsuit is pending.

CONDO INSURANCE

Although the condominium association will likely have a policy to insure the condominium complex, including your condo unit, you should also purchase your own condo insurance policy. A condo policy will insure your personal belongings, and the structural parts of the building that you own, much like a homeowner's policy.

You should obtain a copy of the condominium association's insurance policy to determine what is actually covered in the condo policy. The more you know about the condominium association's insurance the better you will be able to determine what you need to cover in your policy.

Condo Assessment Insurance

Condo owners can also obtain a special type of insurance policy that covers unit "assessment." For example, if a fire damages the lobby of the building, the condo association's policy will cover most of the cost of fixing the damage. However, there may be an additional amount that is not covered by the policy. Generally, this amount is passed on to the condo owners as a "special assessment." Condo unit assessment coverage protect the condo owner in the case this situation arises.

CO-OP INSURANCE

Co-op owners need a special policy (HO-6), which is similar to renter's insurance. Although the corporation generally carries a blanket insurance policy that covers damage to the cooperative property from fire, water, or other disasters, this policy generally does not cover any damage to personal belongings inside your unit. Therefore, additional insurance is recommended to cover your personal possessions.

CHAPTER 8:
THE PLANNED COMMUNITY

WHAT IS A PLANNED COMMUNITY?

A planned community combines certain aspects of the co-op and condo types of ownership. In fact, large portions of the planned communities covenants, conditions and restrictions (CC&R) declarations are indistinguishable from condominium declarations. The only reason planned communities are generally exempt from state and local condominium regulation is that title to the common areas is held in the name of the homeowner association instead of being divided among the unit owners as tenants in common.

For example, in a planned community, the owners hold title to their own single family homes that are located within the development. The common areas of the development—such as the grounds and play areas—belong to an incorporated homeowner association.

Planned communities can vary in size, and can contain both residential and commercial areas. For example, some developments include stores, playgrounds, and other amenities. In some areas, smaller planned communities band together to form a "master " or "umbrella" association for the benefit of the homeowner.

The National Conference of Commissioners on Uniform State Laws drafted the Uniform Planned Community Act, which was approved and recommended for enactment in all states. The Uniform Planned Community Act sets forth guidelines for the creation, alteration and termination of planned communities; management of planned communities; and the protection of purchasers of housing in a planned community.

Selected provisions of the Uniform Planned Community Act are set forth at Appendix 10.

THE HOMEOWNERS ASSOCIATION

Most homeowner associations are corporations established under state common law or not-for-profit corporation law. The homeowner association often performs exactly the same function as condominium associations. They derive their power from a declaration of covenants, conditions and restrictions (CC&R) which is recorded at the beginning of the project.

A homeowner association is similar to other corporations—i.e., it is governed by a board of directors elected by the members and a set of rules called bylaws. Books and records of financial transactions must be kept, taxes paid, and certain services provided to members. Usually the board has an annual budget prepared to estimate expenses, and then assesses each member a share of the costs.

In a planned community, all of the homeowners are required to join the homeowner association. Recent studies demonstrate that approximately one in six people in America—approximately 50 million residents—live in a community regulated by a homeowners association. There is no statute regulating homeowner associations.

The homeowner association is responsible for maintaining the common areas of the development. The homeowners pay periodic assessments for the upkeep and expenses of the common areas.

The typical homeowner's association carries out the following duties:

The homeowner's association collects association dues, imposes special assessments used to finance major improvements and repairs.

The homeowner's association enforces rules.

The homeowner's association fines residents who break the rules.

The homeowner's association can foreclose on properties belonging to owners who do not pay their dues, assessments and fines.

If you are dissatisfied with your homeowner association, e.g., repairs are neglected, you should bring this to the attention of the board. Sometimes all you need to do is place a phone call. If the oral request is ignored, you can write a letter. The letter should be factual, brief and not hostile.

Keep copies of any letters that you send, and notes of telephone conversations, in case the matter is not quickly resolved. An attempt to influence the board is always more persuasive if it is presented by a significant number of members. If your problem is one that others are affected by, it is worth organizing the other members. If you do, and the attempt to change the situation is not successful, the organized group can always seek to elect new directors at the next annual meeting.

If you are unable to resolve your problems with the board, you should hire an attorney who is familiar with handling homeowner association problems. Some lawyers will not charge for a single initial consultation or will charge only a minimal fee. Most lawyers will attempt to resolve any matter through negotiation before considering litigation, as litigation is costly and usually lengthy. Litigating against the board of an homeowner association may be undesirable insofar as these are people with whom you live day-to-day.

MAINTENANCE FEES

In deciding whether to purchase a home in a planned community, it is important to consider the mandatory maintenance fees assessed for the upkeep of the common property. Such fees can become very costly, particularly if the development has recreational facilities, such as a golf course, tennis courts, or a pool. You should find out if there is a cap on how much the maintenance fees can be raised each year, and if there are any special assessments routinely imposed which are above and beyond the regular maintenance fees.

It is also important to find out how much of a reserve fund the association maintains to cover the cost of repairs to common areas, such as pools and tennis courts. Is there enough to cover major repairs without having to charge homeowners a special assessment? Is the homeowners' association involved in any litigation against the builder and if so, what is the status? Be sure to ask to see a copy of the current and last year's association budget, and ask about any history of special assessments.

COVENANTS, CONDITIONS AND RESTRICTIONS (CC&RS)

When you purchase a home in a planned community, you must abide by certain rules set forth by the homeowners association. In fact, the deed to your home will likely include restrictions on how you can use your own property. These restrictions are known collectively as covenants, conditions and restrictions (CC&Rs). A common restriction, for example, requires all homeowners to keep their house painted a certain color.

If you are interested in purchasing a home in a planned community, it is important that you consult an attorney who can go over the deed and the restrictions with you so that you are aware of all of your rights and responsibilities as a homeowner before purchasing the property.

APPENDIX 1:
INTERNAL REVENUE CODE—SECTION 216

I.R.C. §216. DEDUCTION OF TAXES, INTEREST, AND BUSINESS DEPRECIATION BY COOPERATIVE HOUSING CORPORATION TENANT-STOCKHOLDER

(a) Allowance of deduction—In the case of a tenant-stockholder (as defined in subsection (b)(2)), there shall be allowed as a deduction amounts (not otherwise deductible) paid or accrued to a cooperative housing corporation within the taxable year, but only to the extent that such amounts represent the tenant-stockholder's proportionate share of—

(1) the real estate taxes allowable as a deduction to the corporation under section 164 which are paid or incurred by the corporation on the houses or apartment building and on the land on which such houses (or building) are situated, or

(2) the interest allowable as a deduction to the corporation under section 163 which is paid or incurred by the corporation on its indebtedness contracted—

(A) in the acquisition, construction, alteration, rehabilitation, or maintenance of the houses or apartment building, or

(B) in the acquisition of the land on which the houses (or apartment building) are situated.

(b) Definitions—For purposes of this section—

(1) Cooperative housing corporation—The term "cooperative housing corporation" means a corporation—

(A) having one and only one class of stock outstanding,

(B) each of the stockholders of which is entitled, solely by reason of his ownership of stock in the corporation, to occupy for dwelling purposes a house, or an apartment in a building, owned or leased by such corporation,

(C) no stockholder of which is entitled (either conditionally or unconditionally) to receive any distribution not out of earnings and profits of the corporation except on a complete or partial liquidation of the corporation, and

(D) 80 percent or more of the gross income of which for the taxable year in which the taxes and interest described in subsection (a) are paid or incurred is derived from tenant-stockholders.

(2) Tenant-stockholder—The term "tenant-stockholder" means a person who is a stockholder in a cooperative housing corporation, and whose stock is fully paid-up in an amount not less than an amount shown to the satisfaction of the Secretary as bearing a reasonable relationship to the portion of the value of the corporation's equity in the houses or apartment building and the land on which situated which is attributable to the house or apartment which such person is entitled to occupy.

(3) Tenant-stockholder's proportionate share

(A) In general—Except as provided in subparagraph (B), the term "tenant-stockholder's proportionate share" means that proportion which the stock of the cooperative housing corporation owned by the tenant-stockholder is of the total outstanding stock of the corporation (including any stock held by the corporation).

(B) Special rule where allocation of taxes or interest reflect cost to corporation of stockholder's unit

(i) In general—If, for any taxable year—

(I) each dwelling unit owned or leased by a cooperative housing corporation is separately allocated a share of such corporation's real estate taxes described in subsection (a)(1) or a share of such corporation's interest described in subsection (a)(2), and

(II) such allocations reasonably reflect the cost to such corporation of such taxes, or of such interest, attributable to the tenant-stockholder's dwelling unit (and such unit's share of the common areas), then the term "tenant-stockholder's proportionate share" means the shares determined in accordance with the allocations described in subclause (II).

(ii) Election by corporation required—Clause (i) shall apply with respect to any cooperative housing corporation only if such corporation elects its application. Such an election, once made, may be revoked only with the consent of the Secretary.

(4) Stock owned by governmental units—For purposes of this subsection, in determining whether a corporation is a cooperative housing corporation, stock owned and apartments leased by the United States or any of its possessions, a State or any political subdivision thereof, or any agency or instrumentality of the foregoing empowered to acquire shares in a cooperative housing corporation for the purpose of providing housing facilities, shall not be taken into account.

(5) Prior approval of occupancy—For purposes of this section, in the following cases there shall not be taken into account the fact that (by agreement with the cooperative housing corporation) the person or his nominee may not occupy the house or apartment without the prior approval of such corporation:

(A) In any case where a person acquires stock of a cooperative housing corporation by operation of law.

(B) In any case where a person other than an individual acquires stock of a cooperative housing corporation.

(C) In any case where the original seller acquires any stock of the cooperative housing corporation from the corporation not later than 1 year after the date on which the apartments or houses (or leaseholds therein) are transferred by the original seller to the corporation.

(6) Original seller defined For purposes of paragraph (5), the term "original seller" means the person from whom the corporation has acquired the apartments or houses (or leaseholds therein).

(c) Treatment as property subject to depreciation

(1) In general—So much of the stock of a tenant-stockholder in a cooperative housing corporation as is allocable, under regulations prescribed by the Secretary, to a proprietary lease or right of tenancy in property subject to the allowance for depreciation under section 167(a) shall, to the extent such proprietary lease or right of tenancy is used by such tenant-stockholder in a trade or business or for the production of income, be treated as property subject to the allowance for depreciation under section 167(a). The preceding sentence shall not be construed to limit or deny a deduction for depreciation under section 167(a) by a cooperative housing corporation with respect to property owned by such a corporation and leased to tenant-stockholders.

    (2) Deduction limited to adjusted basis in stock

       (A) In general—The amount of any deduction for depreciation allowable under section 167(a) to a tenant-stockholder with respect to any stock for any taxable year by reason of paragraph (1) shall not exceed the adjusted basis of such stock as of the close of the taxable year of the tenant-stockholder in which such deduction was incurred.

       (B) Carryforward of disallowed amount—The amount of any deduction which is not allowed by reason of subparagraph (A) shall, subject to the provisions of subparagraph (A), be treated as a deduction allowable under section 167(a) in the succeeding taxable year.

(d) Disallowance of deduction for certain payments to the corporation—No deduction shall be allowed to a stockholder in a cooperative housing corporation for any amount paid or accrued to such corporation during any taxable year (in excess of the stockholder's proportionate share of the items described in subsections (a)(1) and (a)(2)) to the extent that, under regulations prescribed by the Secretary, such amount is properly allocable to amounts paid or incurred at any time by the corporation which are chargeable to the corporation's capital account. The stockholder's adjusted basis in the stock in the corporation shall be increased by the amount of such disallowance.

(e) Distributions by cooperative housing corporations—Except as provided in regulations no gain or loss shall be recognized on the distribution by a cooperative housing corporation of a dwelling unit to a stockholder in such corporation if such distribution is in exchange for the stockholder's stock in such corporation and such exchange qualifies for nonrecognition of gain under section 1034(f).

APPENDIX 2:
THE NEW YORK CONDOMINIUM ACT

ARTICLE 9-B—CONDOMINIUM ACT

S 339-d. Short title.

This article shall be known and may be cited as the "condominium act."

S 339-e. Definitions.

As used in this article, unless the context otherwise requires:

1. "Building" means a multi-unit building or buildings, or a group of buildings whether or not attached to each other, comprising a part of the property.

2. "Common charges" means each unit's proportionate share of the common expenses in accordance with its common interest.

3. "Common elements," unless otherwise provided in the declaration, means and includes:

(a) The land on which the building is located;

(b) The foundations, columns, girders, beams, supports, main walls, roofs, halls, corridors, lobbies, stairs, stairways, fire escapes, and entrances and exits of the building;

(c) The basements, cellars, yards, gardens, recreational or community facilities, parking areas and storage spaces;

(d) The premises for the lodging or use of janitors and other persons employed for the operation of the property;

(e) Central and appurtenant installations for services such as power, light, gas, hot and cold water, heating, refrigeration, air conditioning and incinerating;

(f) The elevators, escalators, tanks, pumps, motors, fans, compressors, ducts and in general all apparatus and installations existing for common use;

(g) Such facilities as may be designated as common elements in the declaration; and

(h) All other parts of the property necessary or convenient to its existence, maintenance and safety, or normally in common use.

4. "Common expenses" means and includes:

(a) Expenses of operation of the property, and

(b) All sums designated common expenses by or pursuant to the provisions of this article, the declaration or the by-laws.

5. "Common interest" means the (i) proportionate, undivided interest in fee simple absolute, or (ii) proportionate undivided leasehold interest in the common elements appertaining to each unit, as expressed in the declaration.

6. "Common profits" means the excess of all receipts of the rents, profits and revenues from the common elements remaining after the deduction of the common expenses.

7. "Declaration" means the instrument by which the property is submitted to the provisions of this article, as hereinafter provided, and such instrument as from time to time amended, consistent with the provisions of this article and of the by-laws.

8. "Majority" of unit owners means either (i) more than fifty per cent in common interest in the aggregate, or (ii) more than fifty per cent in number of units in the aggregate, or (iii) more than fifty per cent in the aggregate in both common interest and in number of units, as may be specified herein or in the declaration or the by-laws with respect to any matter or matters. Any specified percentage of unit owners means (i) such percentage in common interest in the aggregate, or (ii) such percentage in number of units in the aggregate, or (iii) such percentage in common interest and such percentage in number of units, as may be specified herein or in the declaration or the by-laws with respect to any matter or matters, provided, however, that different percentages in interest and in number of units may be so specified.

9. "Operation of the property" means and includes the administration and operation of the property and the maintenance, repair and replacement of, and the making of any additions and improvements to, the common elements.

10. "Person" means a natural person, corporation, partnership, association, trustee or other legal entity.

11. "Property" means and includes the land, the building and all other improvements thereon, (i) owned in fee simple absolute, or (ii) in the case of a condominium devoted exclusively to non-residential purposes, held under a lease or sublease, or separate unit leases or subleases, the unexpired term or terms of which on the date of recording of the declaration shall not be less than thirty years, or (iii) in the case of a qualified leasehold condominium, held under a lease or sublease, or separate unit leases or subleases, the unexpired term or terms of which on the date of recording of the declaration shall not be less than fifty years, and all easements, rights and appurtenances belonging thereto, and all other property, personal or mixed, intended for use in connection therewith, which have been or are intended to be submitted to the provisions of this article.

12. "Qualified leasehold condominium" means any leasehold interest in real property intended to be used for either residential purposes, commercial purposes, industrial purposes or any combination of such purposes, together with any fee simple absolute or leasehold interest in the buildings and all other improvements which have been or at any time hereafter may be erected upon such real property, which has been or is intended to be submitted to the provisions of this article, provided that, on the date of the recording of the declaration: (i) the battery park city authority or the Roosevelt Island operating corporation is the holder of the tenant's interest in such leasehold interest or (ii) the Queens West development corporation is the holder of the landlord's interest in such leasehold interest.

13. "Recording officer" and "recording" or "recorded" shall have the meanings stated in section two hundred ninety of this chapter.

14. "Unit" means a part of the property intended for any type of use or uses, and with an exit to a public street or highway or to a common element or elements leading to a public street or highway, and may include such appurtenances as garage and other parking space, storage room, balcony, terrace and patio, but in no event may utility facilities such as those for water or sewage treatment or power generation appear as single units.

15. "Unit designation" means the number, letter or combination thereof or other official designations conforming to the tax lot number, if any, designating the unit in the declaration and on the floor plans.

16. "Unit owner" means the person or persons owning a unit in fee simple absolute or, in the case either (i) of a condominium devoted

exclusively to non-residential purposes, or (ii) a qualified leasehold condominium, owning a unit held under a lease or sublease.

§ 339-f. Application of article.

1. This article shall be applicable only to property the sole owner or all the owners of which submit the same to the provisions hereof by duly executing and recording a declaration as hereinafter provided.

2. Such property shall be submitted and subject to the authority of and review by the county planning agency as set forth in section two hundred thirty-nine-n of article twelve-B of the general municipal law, irrespective of and notwithstanding the distance requirement of the second unnumbered paragraph of such section, and as though the property were a subdivision plat subject to such section. This subdivision shall not be applicable to:

(i) property which has received local planning board approval prior to December twenty-first, nineteen hundred seventy-eight; or

(ii) property submitted to the provisions of this article on which any building or buildings or any portion thereof has been rented to any tenant or tenants.

§ 339-g. Status of units.

Each unit, together with its common interest, shall for all purposes constitute real property.

§ 339-h. Ownership of units.

Each unit owner shall be entitled to the exclusive ownership and possession of his unit.

§ 339-i. Common elements.

1. Each unit shall have appurtenant thereto a common interest as expressed in the declaration. Such interest shall be (i) in the approximate proportion that the fair value of the unit at the date of the declaration bears to the then aggregate fair value of all the units or (ii) in the approximate proportion that the floor area of the unit at the date of the declaration bears to the then aggregate floor area of all the units, but such proportion shall reflect the substantially exclusive advantages enjoyed by one or more but not all units in a part or parts of the common elements or (iii) the interest of each of the units shall be in equal percentages, one for each unit as of the date of filing the declaration, or in equal percentages within separate classifications of units as of the date of filing the declaration, or (iv) upon floor space, subject to the location of such space and the additional factors of relative value to other space in the condominium, the uniqueness of the unit, the avail-

ability of common elements for exclusive or shared use, and the overall dimensions of the particular unit.

2. The common interest appurtenant to each unit as expressed in the declaration shall have a permanent character and shall not be altered without the consent of all unit owners affected, expressed in an amended declaration. However, the declaration may contain provisions relating to the appropriation, taking or condemnation by eminent domain by a federal, state or local government, or instrumentality thereof, including, but not limited to, reapportionment or other change of the common interest appurtenant to each unit, or portion thereof, remaining after a partial appropriation, taking or condemnation. The common interest shall not be separated from the unit to which it appertains. Nothing contained in this article shall prohibit the division of any unit and common interest appurtenant thereto in a non-residential unit in the manner permitted by the declaration and bylaws, including changes in the number of rooms; in no case may such division result in a greater percentage of common interest for the total of the new units than existed for the original unit before division. Where authorized by the declaration and bylaws, an appropriate amendment to the declaration may be filed by the new unit owners under the same file number and under procedure set forth in section three hundred thirty-nine-p hereof, and the local tax authorities shall provide and certify upon the proposed amendment a conforming tax lot number upon completion of the new units.

3. The common elements shall remain undivided and no right shall exist to partition or divide any thereof, except as otherwise provided in this article. Any provision to the contrary shall be null and void. Nothing in this subdivision shall be deemed to prevent ownership of a unit by the entireties, jointly or in common.

4. Each unit owner may use the common elements in accordance with the purpose for which they are intended, without hindering the exercise of or encroaching upon the rights of the other unit owners, but this subsection shall not be deemed to prevent some unit or units from enjoying substantially exclusive advantages in a part or parts of the common elements as expressed in the declaration or by-laws.

5. The unit owners shall have the irrevocable right, to be exercised by the board of managers, to have access to each unit from time to time during reasonable hours to the extent necessary for the operation of the property, or for making emergency repairs therein necessary to prevent damage to the common elements or to another unit or units, and the by-laws may contain reasonable rules and regulations for the administration of this provision as the privacy of the units and the pro-

tection of them and their contents from burglary, theft or larceny requires.

S 339-j. Compliance with by-laws and rules and regulations.

Each unit owner shall comply strictly with the by-laws and with rules, regulations, resolutions and decisions adopted pursuant thereto. Failure to comply with any of the same shall be ground for an action to recover sums due, for damages or injunctive relief or both maintainable by the board of managers on behalf of the unit owners or, in a proper case, by an aggrieved unit owner. In any case of flagrant or repeated violation by a unit owner, he may be required by the board of managers to give sufficient surety or sureties for his future compliance with the by-laws, rules, regulations, resolutions and decisions. Notwithstanding the foregoing provisions of this section, no action or proceeding for any relief may be maintained due to the display of a flag of the United States measuring not more than four feet by six feet.

S 339-k. Certain work prohibited.

No unit owner shall do any work which would jeopardize the soundness or safety of the property, reduce the value thereof or impair any easement or hereditament, nor may any unit owner add any material structure or excavate any additional basement or cellar, without in every such case the consent of all the unit owners affected being first obtained.

S 339-l. Liens against common elements; liens against units; liens for labor performed or materials furnished.

1. Subsequent to recording the declaration and while the property remains subject to this article, no lien of any nature shall thereafter arise or be created against the common elements except with the unanimous consent of the unit owners. During such period, liens may arise or be created only against the several units and their respective common interests.

2. Labor performed on or materials furnished to a unit shall not be the basis for the filing of a lien pursuant to article two of the lien law against the unit of any unit owner not expressly consenting to or requesting the same, except in the case of emergency repairs. No labor performed on or materials furnished to the common elements shall be the basis for a lien thereon, but all common charges received and to be received by the board of managers, and the right to receive such funds, shall constitute trust funds for the purpose of paying the cost of such labor or materials performed or furnished at the express request or with the consent of the manager, managing agent or board of manag-

ers, and the same shall be expended first for such purpose before expending any part of the same for any other purpose.

S 339-m. Common profits and expenses.

The common profits of the property shall be distributed among, and the common expenses shall be charged to, the unit owners according to their respective common interests, provided however, that expenses of insurance may be charged as provided in section three hundred thirty-nine-bb. Notwithstanding any provision of this article, profits and expenses may be specially allocated and apportioned by the board of managers in a manner different from common profits and expenses, to one or more non-residential units where so authorized by the declaration and bylaws. In the case of units in any building, residential or non-residential, or a combination thereof, profits and expenses may be specially allocated and apportioned based on special or exclusive use or availability or exclusive control of particular units or common areas by particular unit owners, if so authorized by the declaration and bylaws, in a manner different from common profits and expenses.

S 339-n. Contents of declaration.

The declaration shall contain the following particulars:

1. A statement of intention to submit the property to the provisions of this article.

2. Description of the land on which the building and improvements are or are to be located.

3. Description of the building, including the location of the building by reference to fixed monuments or tax map parcel data, stating the number of stories, basements and cellars, the number of units and the principal materials of which it is or is to be constructed.

4. The unit designation of each unit, and a statement of its location, approximate area, number of rooms in residential areas, and common element to which it has immediate access, and any other data necessary for its proper identification.

5. Description of the common elements and a statement of the common interest of each unit owner.

6. Statement of the uses for which the building and each of the units are intended.

7. A designation of the secretary of state as agent of the corporation or board of managers upon whom process against it may be served. Service of process on the secretary of state as agent of such corporation or board of managers shall be made personally delivering to and

leaving with him or her or his or her deputy, or with any person authorized by the secretary of state to receive such service, at the office of the department of state in the city of Albany, duplicate copies of such process together with the statutory fee, which shall be a taxable disbursement. Service of process on such corporation or board of managers shall be complete when the secretary of state is so served. The secretary of state shall promptly send one of such copies by certified mail, return receipt requested, to such corporation or board of managers, at the post office address, on file in the department of state, specified for such purpose. Nothing in this subdivision shall affect the right to serve process in any other manner permitted by law. The corporation or board of managers shall also file with the secretary of state the name and post office address within or without this state to which the secretary of state shall mail a copy of any process against it served upon the secretary of state and shall update the filing as necessary.

8. Any further details in connection with the property which the person or persons executing the declaration may deem desirable to set forth.

9. The method by which the declaration may be amended, consistent with the provisions of this article.

S 339-o. Contents of deeds and leases of units.

Deeds and leases of units shall include the following particulars:

1. Description of the land as provided in subsection two of section three hundred thirty-nine-n and the liber, page and date of recording of the declaration or solely by naming the city, village or town and the county in which the unit is located and referring to the liber, page and date of recording of the declaration.

2. The unit designation of the unit in the declaration and any other data necessary for its proper identification.

3. Statement of the use for which the unit is intended.

4. The common interest appertaining to the unit.

5. Any further details which the grantor and grantee may deem desirable to set forth.

S 339-p. Copy of floor plans to be filed.

Simultaneously with the recording of the declaration there shall be filed in the office of the recording officer a set of the floor plans of the building showing the layout, locations, and approximate dimensions of the units, stating the declarants' names, and bearing the verified statement of a registered architect or licensed professional engineer certifying that it is an accurate copy of portions of the plans of the building as filed with and approved by the municipal or other governmental subdivision having jurisdiction over the issuance of permits for the construction of buildings. If such floor plans do not contain unit designations certified by the appropriate local tax authorities as conforming to the official tax lot number, there shall be filed in the office of the recording officer prior to the first conveyance of a unit a floor plan containing a unit designation certified by the appropriate local tax authority as conforming to the official tax lot number. It shall be the duty of the appropriate local tax authority to provide such number for each unit upon completion of such unit. If such plans do not include a verified statement by such architect or engineer that such plans fully and fairly depict the layout, location, unit designations and approximate dimensions of any particular unit or units as built, there shall be recorded prior to each first conveyance of such particular unit or units an amendment to the declaration to which shall be attached a verified statement of a registered architect or licensed professional engineer certifying that the plans theretofore filed, or being filed simultaneously with such amendment, fully and fairly depict the layout, location, unit designations and approximate dimensions of the particular unit or units as built. Such plans shall be designated "condominium", assigned a file number and kept on file by the recording officer. Such plans shall be indexed under the names of the declarants and in the block index if any. The record of the declaration shall contain a reference to the file number of the floor plans of the building affected thereby.

S 339-q. Filing with board.

True copies of the floor plans, the declaration, the by-laws and any rules and regulations shall be kept on file in the office of the board of managers and shall be available for inspection at convenient hours of weekdays by persons having an interest.

S 339-r. Blanket mortgages and other blanket liens affecting a unit at time of first conveyance.

At the time of the first conveyance of each unit, every mortgage and other lien affecting such unit and any other unit shall be paid and satisfied of record, or the unit being conveyed and its common interest shall be released therefrom by partial release duly recorded.

S 339-s. Recording.

1. The declaration, any amendment or amendments thereof, and every instrument affecting the property or any unit included within the meaning of "conveyance" as used in article nine of this chapter, shall

be entitled to be indexed and recorded pursuant to and with the same effect as provided in said article nine. The recording officer shall not accept such an instrument constituting a condominium map unless it has endorsed thereon or attached thereto a certificate of the county director of real property tax services that the fee authorized by section five hundred three of the real property tax law, if any, has been paid. Neither the declaration nor any amendment thereof shall be valid unless duly recorded.

2. Each such declaration, and any amendment or amendments thereof shall be filed with the department of state.

S 339-t. Withdrawal from provisions of this article.

If withdrawal of the property from this article is authorized by at least eighty per cent in number and in common interest of the units, or by at least such larger percentage either in number or in common interest, or in both number and common interest, as may be specified in the by-laws, then the property shall be subject to an action for partition by any unit owner or lienor as if owned in common, in which event the net proceeds of sale shall be divided among all the unit owners in proportion to their respective common interests, provided, however, that no payment shall be made to a unit owner until there has first been paid off out of his share of such net proceeds all liens on his unit. Such withdrawal of the property from this article shall not bar its subsequent submission to the provisions of this article in accordance with the terms of this article.

S 339-u. By-laws.

The operation of the property shall be governed by by-laws, a true copy of which shall be annexed to the declaration. No modification of or amendment to the by-laws shall be valid unless set forth in an amendment to the declaration and such amendment is duly recorded.

S 339-v. Contents of by-laws.

1. The by-laws shall provide for at least the following:

(a) The nomination and election of a board of managers, the number of persons constituting the same, and that the terms of at least one-third of the members of such board shall expire annually; the powers and duties of the board; the compensation, if any, of the members of the board; the method of removal from office of members of the board; and whether or not the board may engage the services of a manager or managing agent or both, and specifying which of the powers and duties granted to the board by this article or otherwise may be delegated by the board to either or both of them. Nothing contained herein shall bar the incorporation of the board of managers under applicable statutes of this state; such incorporation must be consistent with the other provisions of this article and the nature of the condominium purpose.

(b) Method of calling meetings of the unit owners; what percentage of the unit owners, if other than a majority, shall constitute a quorum; and what percentage shall, consistent with the provisions of this act, be necessary to adopt decisions binding on all unit owners.

(c) Election of a president from among the board of managers who shall preside over the meetings of such board and of the unit owners.

(d) Election of a secretary who shall keep a record wherein actions of such board and of meetings of the unit owners shall be recorded.

(e) Election of a treasurer who shall keep the financial records and books of account.

(f) Operation of the property, payment of the common expenses and determination and collection of the common charges.

(g) The manner of designation and removal of persons employed for the operation of the property.

(h) Method of adopting and of amending administrative rules and regulations governing the details of the operation and use of the common elements.

(i) Such restrictions on and requirements respecting the use and maintenance of the units and the use of the common elements, not set forth in the declaration, as are designed to prevent unreasonable interference with the use of their respective units and of the common elements by the several unit owners.

(j) The percentage of the unit owners, but not less than sixty-six and two-thirds per cent in number and common interest except in the case where all units are non-residential, which may at any time modify or amend the by-laws.

2. The by-laws may also provide for the following:

(a) Provisions governing the alienation, conveyance, sale, leasing, purchase, ownership and occupancy of units, provided, however, that the by-laws shall contain no provision restricting the alienation, conveyance, sale, leasing, purchase, ownership and occupancy of units because of race, creed, color or national origin.

(b) Provisions governing the payment, collection and disbursement of funds, including reserves, to provide for major and minor maintenance, repairs, additions, improvements, replacements, working capital, bad debts and unpaid common expenses, depreciation, obsolescence and similar purposes.

(c) The form by which the board of managers, acting on behalf of the unit owners, where authorized by this statute or the declaration, may acquire and hold any unit and lease, mortgage and convey the same.

(d) Any other provisions, not inconsistent with the provisions of this article, relating to the operation of the property.

S 339-w. Books of receipts and expenditures; availability for examination.

The manager or board of managers, as the case may be, shall keep detailed, accurate records, in chronological order, of the receipts and expenditures arising from the operation of the property. Such records and the vouchers authorizing the payments shall be available for examination by the unit owners at convenient hours of weekdays. A written report summarizing such receipts and expenditures shall be rendered by the board of managers to all unit owners at least once annually.

S 339-x. Waiver of use of common elements; abandonment of unit; conveyance to board of managers.

No unit owner may exempt himself from liability for his common charges by waiver of the use or enjoyment of any of the common elements or by abandonment of his unit. Subject to such terms and conditions as may be specified in the by-laws, any unit owner may, by conveying his unit and his common interest to the board of managers on behalf of all other unit owners, exempt himself from common charges thereafter accruing.

S 339-y. Separate taxation.

1. (a) With respect to all property submitted to the provisions of this article other than property which is the subject of a qualified leasehold condominium, each unit and its common interest, not including any personal property, shall be deemed to be a parcel and shall be subject to separate assessment and taxation by each assessing unit, school district, special district, county or other taxing unit, for all types of taxes authorized by law including but not limited to special ad valorem levies and special assessments, except that the foregoing shall not apply to a unit held under lease or sublease unless the declaration requires the unit owner to pay all taxes attributable to his unit. Neither the building, the property nor any of the common elements shall be deemed to be a parcel.

(b) In no event shall the aggregate of the assessment of the units plus their common interests exceed the total valuation of the property were the property assessed as a parcel.

(c) For the purposes of this and the next succeeding section the terms "assessing unit", "assessment", "parcel", "special ad valorem levy", "special assessment", "special district", "taxation" and "taxes" shall have the meanings specified in section one hundred two of the real property tax law.

(d) The provisions of paragraph (b) of this subdivision shall not apply to such real property classified within:

(i) on and after January first, nineteen hundred eighty-six, class one of section one thousand eight hundred two of the real property tax law; or

(ii) on and after January first, nineteen hundred eighty-four, the homestead class of an approved assessing unit which has adopted the provisions of section one thousand nine hundred three of the real property tax law, or the homestead class of the portion outside an approved assessing unit of an eligible split school district which has adopted the provisions of section nineteen hundred three-a of the real property tax law; provided, however, that, in an approved assessing unit which adopted the provisions of section one thousand nine hundred three of the real property tax law prior to the effective date of this subdivision, paragraph (b) of this subdivision shall apply to all such real property (i) which is classified within the homestead class pursuant to paragraph one of subdivision (e) of section one thousand nine hundred one of the real property tax law and (ii) which, regardless of classification, was on the assessment roll prior to the effective date of this subdivision unless the governing body of such approved assessing unit provides by local law adopted after a public hearing, prior to the taxable status date of such assessing unit next occurring after December thirty-first, nineteen hundred eighty-three, that such paragraph (b) shall not apply to such real property to which this clause applies. Provided further, however, real property subject to the provisions of this subparagraph shall be assessed pursuant to subdivision two of section five hundred eighty-one of the real property tax law.

(e) On the first assessment roll with a taxable status date on or after the effective date of a declaration filed with the recording officer and on every assessment roll thereafter, the assessor shall enter each unit as a parcel, as provided in paragraph (a) of this subdivision, based upon the condition and ownership of each such unit on the appropriate valuation and taxable status dates. Units owned by a developer may be entered as a single parcel with a parcel description corresponding to the entire development, including the land under such development, and excluding those units appearing separately. Upon the first assessment roll where each unit is separately assessed, only an individual unit and its common interest shall constitute a parcel.

(f) The provisions of paragraph (b) of this subdivision shall not apply to a converted condominium unit in a municipal corporation other than a special assessing unit, which has adopted, prior to the taxable status date of the assessment roll upon which its taxes will be levied, a local law or, for a school district, a resolution providing that the provisions of paragraph (b) of this subdivision shall not apply to a converted condominium unit within that municipal corporation. A converted condominium unit for purposes of this paragraph shall mean a dwelling unit held in condominium form of ownership that has previously been on an assessment roll as a dwelling unit in other than condominium form of ownership, and has not been previously subject to the provisions of paragraph (b) of this subdivision.

2. With respect only to qualified leasehold condominiums:

(a) Each unit, its common interest, not including any personal property, and the proportionate undivided part of the real property which is the subject of a qualified leasehold condominium and is allocated to such unit (as expressed in the declaration), shall be deemed to be a parcel, shall be subject to separate assessment to the unit owner and shall be subject to taxation by each assessing unit, school district, special district, county or other taxing unit for all types of taxes authorized by law including, but not limited to, special ad valorem levies and special assessments. Neither the real property which is the subject of a qualified leasehold condominium, the building, the property nor any of the common elements shall be deemed to be a parcel. In no event shall the aggregate of the assessment of the units plus their common interests plus their proportionate undivided parts (as expressed in the declaration) of said real property exceed the total valuation of the property and said real property assessed as a single parcel owned in fee. No provision of this paragraph shall be deemed to subject to taxation any parcel or part thereof which, pursuant to applicable law, is either exempt from taxation or with respect to which no taxes are payable.

(b) For the purposes of section five hundred two of the real property tax law, both the unit owner and the owner of the real property which is the subject of a qualified leasehold condominium shall be deemed to be the owner of the parcel in which such unit is included; provided, however, that for the purposes of section nine hundred twenty-six of the real property tax law, only the unit owner shall be deemed the owner of the parcel in which such unit is included and only the unit owner shall be personally liable for the payment of any taxes assessed against such parcel. Only the fee owner of the land which is the subject of a qualified leasehold condominium, however, shall be deemed to be the owner of the parcel in which a unit is included for the purposes of determining whether such parcel is subject to or exempt from taxation or whether no taxes are payable with respect thereto.

(c) The taxes assessed against each unit, its common interest and the proportionate undivided part of the real property which is the subject of a qualified leasehold condominium allocated to such unit (as expressed in the declaration), shall constitute a lien solely on that unit, its common interest and the proportionate undivided part of said real property allocated to such unit (as expressed in the declaration), and such taxes shall not constitute a lien on any other unit or the common interest of any other unit or the proportionate undivided part of said real property allocated to any other unit (as expressed in the declaration).

(d) At such time as the real property which is the subject of a qualified leasehold condominium is submitted to the provisions of this article, the assessing unit shall make provision so that the real property which (i) is not the subject of a qualified leasehold condominium and (ii) immediately prior to such submission was included in a parcel in which there also was included all or any part of the real property which is (immediately subsequent to such submission) the subject of a qualified leasehold condominium, is established as a single parcel on the assessment roll and tax map of such assessing unit, separate and apart from any real property which is the subject of a qualified leasehold condominium.

3. All provisions of a declaration relating to a unit, its common interest and the proportionate undivided part of the real property which is the subject of a qualified leasehold condominium allocated to such unit (as expressed in the declaration), which has been sold for taxes shall survive and shall be enforceable after the issuance of a tax deed for such unit to the same extent that such provisions would be enforceable against a voluntary grantee of such unit immediately prior to the delivery of such tax deed.

4. The board of managers may act as an agent of each unit owner who has given his written authorization to seek administrative and judicial review of an assessment made in accordance with subdivision one of this section, pursuant to title one-A of article five and title one of article seven of the real property tax law. The board of managers may retain legal counsel on behalf of all unit owners for which it is acting as

agent and to charge all such unit owners a pro rata share of expenses, disbursements and legal fees for which charges the board of managers shall have a lien pursuant to section three hundred thirty-nine-z.

5. Notwithstanding the provisions of any general, special or local law to the contrary, in a city having a population of one million or more, the board of managers shall be authorized to act as the sole agent on behalf of all unit owners, without authorization of each unit owner, for the limited purpose of determining whether or not to waive prospectively the benefit of real property tax abatement and exemption for the property in order to qualify for a partial abatement of real property taxes pursuant to section four hundred sixty-seven-a of the real property tax law.

S 339-z. Lien for common charges; priority; exoneration of grantor and grantee.

The board of managers, on behalf of the unit owners, shall have a lien on each unit for the unpaid common charges thereof, together with interest thereon, prior to all other liens except only (i) liens for taxes on the unit in favor of any assessing unit, school district, special district, county or other taxing unit, (ii) all sums unpaid on a first mortgage of record, and (iii) all sums unpaid on a subordinate mortgage of record held by the New York job development authority, the New York state urban development corporation, the New York city housing development corporation, or in a city having a population of one million or more, the department of housing, preservation and development. Upon the sale or conveyance of a unit, such unpaid common charges shall be paid out of the sale proceeds or by the grantee. Any grantor or grantee of a unit shall be entitled to a statement from the manager or board of managers, setting forth the amount of the unpaid common charges accrued against the unit, and neither such grantor nor grantee shall be liable for, nor shall the unit conveyed be subject to a lien for, any unpaid common charges against such unit accrued prior to such conveyance in excess of the amount therein set forth. Notwithstanding the above, the declaration of an exclusive non-residential condominium may provide that the lien for common charges will be superior to any mortgage liens of record.

S 339-aa. Lien for common charges; duration; foreclosure.

The lien provided for in the immediately preceding section shall be effective from and after the filing in the office of the recording officer in which the declaration is filed a verified notice of lien stating the name (if any) and address of the property, the liber and page of record of the declaration, the name of the record owner of the unit, the unit designation, the amount and purpose for which due, and the date when due;

and shall continue in effect until all sums secured thereby, with the interest thereon, shall have been fully paid or until expiration six years from the date of filing, whichever occurs sooner. In the event that unpaid common charges are due, any member of the board of managers may file a notice of lien as described herein if no notice of lien has been filed within sixty days after the unpaid charges are due. Upon such payment the unit owner shall be entitled to an instrument duly executed and acknowledged certifying to the fact of payment. Such lien may be foreclosed by suit authorized by and brought in the name of the board of managers, acting on behalf of the unit owners, in like manner as a mortgage of real property, without the necessity, however, of naming as a party defendant any person solely by reason of his owning a common interest with respect to the property. In any such foreclosure the unit owner shall be required to pay a reasonable rental for the unit for any period prior to sale pursuant to judgment of foreclosure and sale, if so provided in the by-laws, and the plaintiff in such foreclosure shall be entitled to the appointment of a receiver to collect the same. The board of managers, acting on behalf of the unit owners, shall have power, unless prohibited by the by-laws, to bid in the unit at foreclosure sale, and to acquire and hold, lease, mortgage and convey the same. Suit to recover a money judgment for unpaid common charges shall be maintainable without foreclosing or waiving the lien securing the same, and foreclosure shall be maintainable notwithstanding the pendency of suit to recover a money judgment. Notwithstanding any other provision of this article, if a municipal corporation acquires title to a unit as a result of tax enforcement proceedings, such municipal corporation shall not be liable for and shall not be subject to suit for recovery of the common charges applicable to such unit during the period while title to such unit is held by the municipal corporation or for the payment of any rental for the unit under the provisions of this section, except to the extent of any rent arising from such unit received by such municipal corporation during such period. Except as herein specifically provided, nothing contained herein shall affect or impair or release the unit from the lien for such common charges or impair or diminish the rights of the manager or the board of managers on behalf of the unit owners under this section and section three hundred thirty-nine-z.

S 339-bb. Insurance.

The board of managers shall, if required by the declaration, the by-laws or by a majority of the unit owners, insure the building against loss or damage by fire and such other hazards as shall be required, and shall give written notice of such insurance and of any change therein or termination thereof to each unit owner. In the case of a qualified leasehold condominium, such insurance shall be required in any event, and shall be in an amount equal to full replacement cost of the building. The policy or policies of such insurance shall be updated annually to maintain such insurance in such amount. Nothing herein shall prejudice the right of each unit owner to insure his own unit for his own benefit. The premiums for such insurance on the building shall be deemed common expenses, provided, however, that in charging the same to the unit owners consideration may be given to the higher premium rates on some units than on others.

S 339-cc. Repair or reconstruction.

1. Except as hereinafter provided, damage to or destruction of the building shall be promptly repaired and reconstructed by the board of managers, using the proceeds of insurance, if any, on the building for that purpose, and any deficiency shall constitute common expenses; provided, however, that if three-fourths or more of the building is destroyed or substantially damaged and seventy-five per cent or more of the unit owners do not duly and promptly resolve to proceed with repair or restoration, then and in that event the property or so much thereof as shall remain, shall be subject to an action for partition at the suit of any unit owner or lienor as if owned in common, in which event the net proceeds of sale, together with the net proceeds of insurance policies, if any, shall be considered as one fund and shall be divided among all the unit owners in proportion to their respective common interests, provided, however, that no payment shall be made to a unit owner until there has first been paid off out of his share of such fund all liens on his unit.

2. Notwithstanding the provisions of subdivision one hereof, in the case of a qualified leasehold condominium, any damage to or destruction of the building shall be promptly repaired and reconstructed by the board of managers, and the proceeds of the insurance policy or policies required for qualified leasehold condominiums pursuant to the provisions of section three hundred thirty-nine-bb of this chapter shall first be applied to such repair and reconstruction.

S 339-dd. Actions.

Actions may be brought or proceedings instituted by the board of managers in its discretion, on behalf of two or more of the unit owners, as their respective interests may appear, with respect to any cause of action relating to the common elements or more than one unit. Service of process on the unit owners in any action relating to the common elements or more than one unit may be made on the person designated in the declaration to receive service of process.

S 339-ee. Effect of other laws.

1. All units of a property which shall be submitted to the provisions of this article shall be deemed to be cooperative interests in realty within the meaning of section three hundred fifty-two-e of the general business law. Article nine-A of this chapter shall not apply to the property or any unit. Article eleven of the tax law shall not apply to declarations or any lien for common charges provided for in this article. Any provision of the multiple dwelling law, the multiple residence law, or any state building construction code as to multiple residences pursuant to the provisions of article eighteen of the executive law, requiring registration by the owner or other person having control of a multiple dwelling shall be deemed satisfied in the case of a property submitted to the provisions of this article by registration of the board of managers, such registration to include the name of each unit owner and the designation of his or her unit; each unit owner shall be deemed the person in control of the unit owned by him or her, and the board of managers shall be deemed the person in control of the common elements, for purposes of enforcement of any such law or code, provided, however, that all other provisions of the multiple dwelling law or multiple residence law, otherwise applicable, shall be in full force and effect, and provided further that in a city with a population of one million or more persons registration required by a housing maintenance code of such city shall be deemed satisfied in the case of a property submitted to the provisions of this article by registration of the board of managers which need not include the name of each unit owner and the designation of his or her unit.

2. In the event the proceeds of a construction mortgage were applied to construction of a unit of a condominium submitted to the provisions of this article, or in the event that a unit submitted to the provisions of this act was subject to a blanket mortgage whose proceeds were applied exclusively to payment of the construction mortgage or to capital expenditures or expenses for the development or operation of the condominium, or to purchase of land or buildings for the condominium provided that such purchase was no more than two years prior to the recording of the declaration of condominium, and a mortgage recording tax was duly paid on such construction or blanket mortgage in accordance with article eleven of the tax law, then, as each unit is first conveyed, there shall be allowed a credit against the mortgage recording taxes (except the special additional mortgage recording tax imposed by subdivision one-a of section two hundred fifty-three of the tax law) that would otherwise be payable on a purchase money mortgage, said credit to be in the amount resulting from the product of the purchaser's pro rata percentage of interest in the common elements

and the mortgage tax already paid on the construction or blanket mortgage. No credit shall be allowed under this subdivision (a) on account of the special additional mortgage recording tax imposed by subdivision one-a of section two hundred fifty-three of the tax law or (b) where the first condominium unit is sold more than two years after the construction or blanket mortgage was recorded.

3. Unless specifically exempted by a provision of this article, all property subject to the provisions of this article shall continue to be subject to all laws, rules and resolutions adopted by any county, city, town or village for the health, safety and welfare of its inhabitants or for regulation of the use of real property. Every county, city, town and village shall continue to have all enforcement powers created by such laws, rules or resolutions or the enabling acts of such laws, rules and resolutions and may exercise those enforcement powers against any violation involving property subject to the provisions of this article.

4. Any estimate of tax liability required by any rule adopted pursuant to this article shall not be binding upon any municipality or public official and any document containing such an estimate shall contain a notice to that effect.

S 339-ff. Mortgage investments on units by state agencies, insurers, banking organizations and fiduciaries; limitation to first mortgages.

(a) The following persons: (1) public officers, bodies of the state, municipalities, and municipal subdivisions, (2) persons doing an insurance business (as defined by section one thousand one hundred one of the insurance law), (3) banking organizations (as defined by section two of the banking law), and (4) executors, administrators, trustees, guardians and other fiduciaries, are authorized to invest in bonds, notes and evidences of indebtedness which are secured by first mortgages or deeds of trust upon units and the appurtenant common interests, wherever such persons may invest, and subject to all of the rules and limitations applicable to such investment, in bonds, notes and evidences of indebtedness which are secured by first mortgages or deeds of trust upon real estate. Where the applicable limitations are dependent upon the type of use of the real estate, only the type of use of the particular unit or units which constitute the security for such investment shall be taken into consideration for the purpose of such limitations. The existence of any prior lien for taxes, assessments or other similar charges not yet delinquent shall be disregarded in determining whether a mortgage or deed of trust is a first mortgage or deed of trust.

(b) No person enumerated in subdivision (a) of this section may invest in bonds, notes or evidences of indebtedness secured by mortgages or deeds of trust upon units and the appurtenant common interests, which are other than first mortgages or deeds of trust thereupon, notwithstanding any other provision of law (including section three hundred thirty-nine-g of this chapter).

(c) Notwithstanding subdivisions (a) and (b), banking organizations are authorized, subject to the rules and limitations applicable thereto contained in subdivision four-a of section one hundred three, subdivision six-a of section two hundred thirty-five, subdivision four-a of section three hundred eighty and subdivision eight of section four hundred fifty-six of the banking law, and the New York job development authority is authorized to invest in bonds, notes and evidences of indebtedness which are secured by mortgages other than first mortgages upon units and the appurtenant common interests, provided such mortgages are in compliance with title eight of article eight of the public authorities law.

(d) Notwithstanding subdivisions (a) and (b) of this section, the New York state urban development corporation is authorized to invest in bonds, notes and evidences of indebtedness which are secured by mortgages other than first mortgages upon units and the appurtenant common interests, provided that (i) such units are owned or are to be acquired by a corporation as defined in subparagraph five of paragraph (a) of section one hundred two of the not-for-profit corporation law and are to be used for commercial purposes, and such corporation has executed a loan authorization agreement with the New York state urban development corporation on or before June thirtieth, nineteen hundred eighty-eight or (ii) such units are developed as a part of a project of the New York state urban development corporation that received specific authorization in chapter eight hundred thirty-nine of the laws of nineteen hundred eighty-seven; and further provided that such investments and subordinate mortgages are in compliance with chapter one hundred seventy-four of the laws of nineteen hundred sixty-eight, as subsequently amended.

(e) Notwithstanding subdivisions (a) and (b) of this section, the New York city housing development corporation and a city having a population of one million or more are authorized to invest in bonds, notes, and evidences of indebtedness which are secured by mortgages other than first mortgages upon dwelling units and the appurtenant common interests provided that such investment is made in connection with a project undertaken pursuant to the private housing finance law or the general municipal law.

S 339-gg. Severability.

If any provision of this article or any section, sentence, clause, phrase or word, or the application thereof in any circumstance is held invalid, the validity of the remainder of the article and of the application of any such provision, section, sentence, clause, phrase or word in any other circumstances shall not be affected thereby.

S 339-hh. Reservation of power.

The legislature reserves the right to alter, amend, suspend or repeal in whole or in part this article. Any such change in this article shall be effective notwithstanding any provisions of any declaration or by-laws.

S 339-ii. Construction.

This article shall be liberally construed to effect the purposes thereof.

S 339-jj. Borrowing by board of managers.

1. To the extent authorized by the declaration or the by-laws, the board of managers, on behalf of the unit owners, may incur debt. In addition, subject to any limitations set forth in the declaration or the by-laws, the board of managers, on behalf of the unit owners, may incur debt for any of the purposes enumerated in paragraph (b) of subdivision two of section three hundred thirty-nine-v of this article, provided that (a) such debt is incurred no earlier than the fifth anniversary of the first conveyance of a unit and (b) the incurrence of such debt shall require the consent of a majority in common interest of the unit owners.

2. In connection with a debt incurred by it, the board of managers, on behalf of the unit owners, may (a) assign the rights in and to receive future income and common charges, (b) create a security interest in, assign, pledge, mortgage or otherwise encumber funds or other real or personal property that it holds, (c) agree that, to the extent of any amounts due under any of the provisions of the agreements under which the debt was incurred and subject to the provisions of subdivision two of section three hundred thirty-nine-l of this article, all common charges received and to be received by it, and the right to receive such funds, shall constitute trust funds for the purpose of paying such debt and the same shall be expended for such purpose before expending any part of the same for any other purpose, and (d) agree that at the lender's direction it will increase common charges to the extent necessary to pay any amount when due under any of the provisions of the agreements under which the debt was incurred. The preceding sentence shall not be construed to authorize the board of managers to create a lien on the common elements. Any such assignment may provide that, in the event of a default, the lender shall have the right of the board of managers to file liens in the lender's name on units for unpaid common charges pursuant to sections three hundred thirty-nine-z and three hundred thirty-nine-aa of this article and the right to foreclose

such liens pursuant to section three hundred thirty-nine-aa of this article.

3. Nothing in this section shall impair rights under any loan or other agreement existing prior to the effective date of this section or limit any right or power that a board of managers would otherwise have.

S 339-kk. Rents.

(a) For the purposes of this section, "non-occupying owner" shall mean a unit owner in a condominium association who does not occupy the dwelling unit.

(b) If a non-occupying owner rents any dwelling unit to a rental tenant and then fails to make payments due for common charges, assessments or late fees for such unit within sixty days of the expiration of any grace period after they are due, upon notice in accordance with subdivision (c) of this section, all rental payments from the tenant shall be directly payable to the condominium association.

(c) If the common charges, assessments or late fees due for any unit have not been paid in full, within sixty days after the expiration of any grace period of the earliest due date, the board of managers shall provide written notice to the tenant and the non-occupying owner providing that, commencing immediately and until such time as all payments for common charges, assessments or late fees are made current, all rental payments due subsequent to the issuance of such notice are to be made payable to the condominium association at the address listed on the notice. Where a majority of the board of managers has been elected by and from among the unit owners who are in occupancy, the board may elect not to require that rental payments be made payable to the condominium association. At such time as payments for common charges, assessments and late fees from the non-occupying owner are once again current, notice of such fact shall be given within three business days to the rental tenant and non-occupying owner. Thereafter all rental payments shall be made payable to the non-occupying owner or a designated agent. A non-occupying owner who disputes the association's claim to rental payments pursuant to this section shall be entitled to present facts supporting such owner's position at the next scheduled meeting of the board of managers, which must be held within thirty days of the date that such board receives notice that such owner seeks to dispute such claim.

(d) Nothing in this section shall limit any rights of unit owners or of the board of managers existing under any other law or agreement.

(e) Payment by a rental tenant to the condominium association made in connection with this section shall relieve that rental tenant from the obligation to pay such rent to the non-occupying owner and shall be an absolute defense in any non-payment proceeding commenced by such non-occupying owner against such tenant for such rent.

APPENDIX 3:
SAMPLE CONDOMINIUM FINE POLICY

NAME OF CONDOMINIUM ASSOCIATION:

RULES AND REGULATIONS

FINE POLICY—ASSESSMENT OF FINES.

The violation by any Co-owner, occupant or guest of any of the provisions of the Condominium Documents (Master Deed, Bylaws or Rules and Regulations of the Association) shall be grounds for assessment by the Association, acting through its duly constituted Board of Directors, of monetary fines against the involved Co-owner.

Such Co-owner shall be deemed responsible for such violations whether they occur as a result of his personal actions or the actions of his family, guests, tenants or any other person admitted through such Co-owner to the Condominium Premises.

Upon any such violation being alleged by the Board, the following procedures will be followed:

A. Notice of the violation, including the Condominium Document provision violated, together with a description of the factual nature of the alleged offense set forth with such reasonable specificity as will place the Co-owner on notice as to the violation, shall be sent by first class mail, postage prepaid, or personally delivered to the representative of said Co-owner at the address as shown in the notice required to be filed with the Association pursuant to Article I, Section 3E, of the Restated Condominium Bylaws of [Name of Condominium Association].

B. The offending Co-owner shall be notified of a scheduled hearing before the Board at which the Co-owner may offer evidence in defense of the alleged violation. The appearance before the Board shall be at its next scheduled meeting, but in no event shall the Co-owner be required to appear less than 7 days from the date of the notice.

C. Failure to respond to the notice of violation or appear at the hearing constitutes a default.

D. Upon appearance by the Co-owner before the Board and presentation of evidence of defense, or, in the event of the Co-owner's default, the Board shall by majority vote of a quorum of the Board, decide whether a violation has occurred. The Board's decision is final.

SCHEDULE OF FINES

Upon violation of any of the provisions of the Condominium Documents and after default of the offending Co-owner or upon the decision of the Board as recited above, the following fines shall be levied:

First violation: Warning; no fine shall be levied.

Second Violation: A fine of $25.00 shall be levied.

Third Violation: A fine of $50.00 shall be levied.

Fourth Violation and Each Subsequent Violation: A fine of $100.00 shall be levied.

The Board of Directors, without the necessity of an amendment to the Restated Condominium Bylaws of [Name of Condominium Association], may make such changes in said fines or adopt alternative fines, including the indexing of such fines to the rate of inflation, in accordance with duly adopted Rules and Regulations promulgated in accordance with Article VI, Section 5 of the Restated Condominium Bylaws of [Name of Condominium Association]. For purposes of this Rule, the number of the violation (i.e., first, second, etc.) is determined with respect to the number of times that a Co-owner violates the same provision of the Condominium Documents, as long as that Co-owner may be an owner of a Unit or occupant of the Project, and is not based upon time or violations of entirely different provisions. In the case of continuing violations, a new violation will be deemed to occur each successive week during which a violation continues. Nothing in this Article shall be construed as to prevent the Association from pursuing any other remedy under the Condominium Documents and/or the [State] Condominium Act for such violations, or from combining a fine with any other remedy or requirement to redress any violation.

COLLECTION OF FINES

The fines levied pursuant to the above stated rules and regulations shall be assessed against the co-owner and shall be due and payable together with the regular monthly installment of the Annual Assess-

---

ment next becoming due on the first day of the following month. Failure to pay the fine will subject the Co-owner to all liabilities set forth in the Condominium Documents, including without limitations, those described in Article II and Article XI of the Restated Condominium Bylaws of [Name of Condominium Association]. All unpaid amounts shall further constitute a lien on the Co-owner's unit, enforceable as set forth in Article II of the Restated Condominium Bylaws of [Name of Condominium Association].

APPENDIX 4:
COMPARISON CHART—CO-OP
OWNERSHIP VS. CONDO OWNERSHIP

PROVISION	CO-OP	CONDO
BOARD APPROVAL	Resident/owners can accept or reject applicants	Generally not required
COSTS	Monthly maintenance fee that consists of building upkeep, real estate taxes and payment of underlying co-op loan, a portion of which is tax deductible	Monthly common charges that consist of building upkeep, generally not tax deductible.
FINANCIALS	Prepared annually to determine financial status and profitability of co-op corporation	Prepared annually to determine financial status and profitability of condo association
FINANCING	Generally there are financing restrictions	Only restrictions would be those required by lender
FORM OF OWNERSHIP	Shares of stock in a corporation that owns the building. No deed. Proprietary Lease establishes terms of occupancy	Deed that is recorded and transferable as any other house or property
MANAGEMENT COMPANY	Small buildings are generally self-managed by residents/owners, larger buildings generally managed by outside company that collects maintenance, maintains records, and operates the building	Small buildings are generally self-managed by residents/owners, larger buildings generally managed by outside company that collects maintenance, maintains records, and operates the building, maintains records

PROVISION	CO-OP	CONDO
PROSPECTUS/OFFER-ING PLAN	Outlines terms of original co-op offering and amendments along with rules of the building	Outlines the terms of the original condo offering and amendments along with rules of the building
REAL ESTATE TAXES	Included in co-op maintenance fee	Condo owner pays their own real estate taxes for unit
RIGHT TO SUBLET	Generally requires board approval and subject to time limitation	Generally no restrictions
SALE	Certain co-ops have a transfer fee/flip tax that seller must pay back to the co-op upon sale of the unit	No restrictions and generally no costs.

APPENDIX 5:
HUD CHECKLIST—HOUSING CRITERIA

The Basics

1. What part of town (or country) do you want to live in? _____

2. What price range would you consider? No less than _____ but no more than _____

3. Are schools a factor and, if so, what do you need to take into consideration (e.g., want specific school system, want kids to be able to walk to school, etc.)?
_____

4. Do you want an older home or a newer home (less than 5 years old)? _____

5. What kind of houses would you be willing to see?

    _____One story _____2 story _____split foyer _____bi-level _____tri-level
    _____townhouse or condo _____mobile home

6. What style house appeals to you most?

    ___contemporary ___traditional ___southwestern ___colonial ___no preference

7. How much renovation would you be willing to do? A lot ____ A little ____ None! ____

8. Do you have to be close to public transportation? _____yes _____no

9. Do you have any physical needs that must be met, such as wheelchair access? _____yes
    _____no

10. Do you have any animals that will require special facilities? _____yes _____no

    If so, what? _____

11. The Lot

	Must Have	Would Like to Have	
Large yard (1 acre or more)	_____	_____	
Small yard (less than 1 acre)	_____	_____	
Fenced yard	_____	_____	
Garage	_____	_____	
Carport	_____	_____	
Patio/deck	_____	_____	
Pool	_____	_____	
Outdoor spa	_____	_____	
Extra parking	_____	_____	
Other buildings (barn, shed, etc.)	_____	_____	
Special view	_____	_____	Of what? _____

The Interior

12. How many bedrooms *must* you have? _____ would you like to have? _____

13. How many bathrooms do you want? _____

14. How big would you like your house to be (square feet)? No less than ____
But no more than ____

15. What features do you want to have in your house?

	Must have	Would Like to Have
Air conditioning	____	____
Wall-to-wall carpet	____	____
Ceramic tile	____	____
Hardwood floors	____	____
Eat-in kitchen	____	____
Separate dining room	____	____
Formal living room	____	____
Family room	____	____
Greatroom	____	____
Separate den or library	____	____
Basement	____	____
Separate laundry room	____	____
Fireplace	____	____
Workshop	____	____
No interior steps	____	____
"In-law" apartment	____	____
Spa in bathroom	____	____
Lots of windows (light)	____	____

Community features

16. Do you want to live in an area with a Community Association? ____yes ____no

17. What else do you want in your community?

	Must have	Would like to have
Community pool	____	____
Golf course	____	____
Basketball court	____	____
Tennis courts	____	____
Gated community or doorman	____	____
Clubhouse/activities	____	____

18. Are there any other special features or needs that you must consider when you're looking for a home?

APPENDIX 6:
HUD CHECKLIST—EVALUATING
PROSPECTIVE HOUSING

You'll want to make several copies of this checklist and fill one out for each home you tour. Then, comparing your ratings later will be easy.

THE HOME	Good	Average	Poor
Square footage			
Number of bedrooms			
Number of baths			
Practicality of floorplan			
Interior walls condition			
Closet/storage space			
Basement			
Fireplace			
Cable TV			
Basement: dampness or odors			
Exterior appearance, condition			
Lawn/yard space			
Fence			
Patio or deck			
Garage			
Energy efficiency			
Screens, storm windows			
Roof: age and condition			
Gutters and downspouts			

THE NEIGHBORHOOD	Good	Average	Poor
Appearance/condition of nearby homes/businesses			
Traffic			
Noise Level			
Safety/Security			
Age mix of inhabitants			
Number of children			
Pet restrictions			

THE NEIGHBORHOOD (Cont.)	Good	Average	Poor
Parking			
Zoning regulations			
Neighborhood restrictions/ covenants			
Fire protection			
Police			
Snow removal			
Garbage service			

SCHOOLS	Good	Average	Poor
Age/condition			
Reputation			
Quality of teachers			
Achievement test scores			
Play areas			
Curriculum			
Class size			
Busing distance			

CONVENIENCE TO:	Good	Average	Poor
Supermarket			
Schools			
Work			
Shopping			
Child care			
Hospitals			
Doctor/dentist			
Recreation/parks			
Restaurants/entertainment			
Church/synagogue			
Airport			
Highways			
Public transportation			

APPENDIX 7:
LIST OF QUESTIONS—CO-OP/CONDO
BUYER

1. How many units are there?

2. How many units are occupied?

3. Of the occupied units, what is the ratio between owner-occupied units versus rental tenants?

4. Are the maintenance fees/common charges being paid by the owners in a timely manner? This is important to assess the financial stability of the development.

5. How much are the monthly maintenance fees/common charges for the unit you are considering purchasing?

6. What do the monthly maintenance fees/common charges represent?

7. When are the monthly maintenance fees/common charges due?

8. What has the monthly maintenance fee/common charge for the unit you are considering purchasing averaged over the past 5 years?

9. Does the seller owe any fees and, if so, are there any liens against the unit you are interested in purchasing?

10. Does the monthly maintenance fee/common charge include fees assessed for parking, or the use of recreational facilities, such as the pool or tennis courts, or is the owner responsible for paying these fees separately?

11. If the owner is responsible for these fees, how much are they and when are they due?

12. Are there any restrictions on the use and occupancy of my unit? If so, what are they?

13. Are there any restrictions on subletting my unit? If so, what are they?

14. How much of a reserve is there for upkeep and repairs, if needed? The co-op board/condo association should keep a reserve fund for general operating expenses, and a reserve fund for repairs. Without a reserve fund, the co-op/condo owners could be subjected to special emergency assessments.

15. What repairs are anticipated over the next 5 years? If there is a budget, ask to see a copy.

16. Are the minutes of the co-op board/condo association meetings available for review? If so, ask to see a copy.

17. Ask for a copy of the certificate of insurance for the property so you can review the coverage. Is the development located in a known flood area and, if so, is there adequate insurance coverage?

18. Does the co-op board/condo association keep the owners informed of proposed actions, and do they solicit their opinions concerning decisions on important matters affecting the development? For example, does the board/association hold periodic meetings, distribute a newsletter, or send e-mail messages to owners? An open line of communication is essential to effectively manage a common interest community.

19. Do owners have any voting rights? If so, what are they?

20. Are there any lawsuits pending or anticipated either by or against the board/association? If so, find out what claims are involved in the lawsuit.

APPENDIX 8:
THE FAIR HOUSING ACT

SEC. 800. [42 U.S.C. 3601 NOTE] SHORT TITLE

This title may be cited as the "Fair Housing Act".

SEC. 801. [42 U.S.C. 3601] DECLARATION OF POLICY

It is the policy of the United States to provide, within constitutional limitations, for fair housing throughout the United States.

SEC. 802. [42 U.S.C. 3602] DEFINITIONS

As used in this subchapter—

(a) "Secretary" means the Secretary of Housing and Urban Development.

(b) "Dwelling" means any building, structure, or portion thereof which is occupied as, or designed or intended for occupancy as, a residence by one or more families, and any vacant land which is offered for sale or lease for the construction or location thereon of any such building, structure, or portion thereof.

(c) "Family" includes a single individual.

(d) "Person" includes one or more individuals, corporations, partnerships, associations, labor organizations, legal representatives, mutual companies, joint-stock companies, trusts, unincorporated organizations, trustees, trustees in cases under title 11 [of the United States Code], receivers, and fiduciaries.

(e) "To rent" includes to lease, to sublease, to let and otherwise to grant for a consideration the right to occupy premises not owned by the occupant.

(f) "Discriminatory housing practice" means an act that is unlawful under section 804, 805, 806, or 818 of this title.

(g) "State" means any of the several States, the District of Columbia, the Commonwealth of Puerto Rico, or any of the territories and possessions of the United States.

(h) "Handicap" means, with respect to a person—

(1) a physical or mental impairment which substantially limits one or more of such person's major life activities,

(2) a record of having such an impairment, or

(3) being regarded as having such an impairment, but such term does not include current, illegal use of or addiction to a controlled substance (as defined in section 102 of the Controlled Substances Act (21 U.S.C. 802)).

(i) "Aggrieved person" includes any person who—

(1) claims to have been injured by a discriminatory housing practice; or

(2) believes that such person will be injured by a discriminatory housing practice that is about to occur.

(j) "Complainant" means the person (including the Secretary) who files a complaint under section 810.

(k) "Familial status" means one or more individuals (who have not attained the age of 18 years) being domiciled with—

(1) a parent or another person having legal custody of such individual or individuals; or

(2) the designee of such parent or other person having such custody, with the written permission of such parent or other person.

The protections afforded against discrimination on the basis of familial status shall apply to any person who is pregnant or is in the process of securing legal custody of any individual who has not attained the age of 18 years.

(l) "Conciliation" means the attempted resolution of issues raised by a complaint, or by the investigation of such complaint, through informal negotiations involving the aggrieved person, the respondent, and the Secretary.

(m) "Conciliation agreement" means a written agreement setting forth the resolution of the issues in conciliation.

(n) "Respondent" means—

(1) the person or other entity accused in a complaint of an unfair housing practice; and

(2) any other person or entity identified in the course of investigation and notified as required with respect to respondents so identified under section 810(a).

(o) "Prevailing party" has the same meaning as such term has in section 722 of the Revised Statutes of the United States (42 U.S.C. 1988).

[42 U.S.C. 3602 note] Neither the term "individual with handicaps" nor the term "handicap" shall apply to an individual solely because that individual is a transvestite.

SEC. 803. [42 U.S.C. 3603] EFFECTIVE DATES OF CERTAIN PROHIBITIONS

(a) Subject to the provisions of subsection (b) of this section and section 807 of this title, the prohibitions against discrimination in the sale or rental of housing set forth in section 804 of this title shall apply:

(1) Upon enactment of this subchapter, to—

(A) dwellings owned or operated by the Federal Government;

(B) dwellings provided in whole or in part with the aid of loans, advances, grants, or contributions made by the Federal Government, under agreements entered into after November 20, 1962, unless payment due thereon has been made in full prior to April 11, 1968;

(C) dwellings provided in whole or in part by loans insured, guaranteed, or otherwise secured by the credit of the Federal Government, under agreements entered into after November 20, 1962, unless payment thereon has been made in full prior to April 11, 1968: Provided, That nothing contained in subparagraphs (B) and (C) of this subsection shall be applicable to dwellings solely by virtue of the fact that they are subject to mortgages held by an FDIC or FSLIC institution; and

(D) dwellings provided by the development or the redevelopment of real property purchased, rented, or otherwise obtained from a State or local public agency receiving Federal financial assistance for slum clearance or urban renewal with respect to such real property under loan or grant contracts entered into after November 20, 1962.

(2) After December 31, 1968, to all dwellings covered by paragraph (1) and to all other dwellings except as exempted by subsection (b) of this section.

(b) Nothing in section 804 of this title (other than subsection (c)) shall apply to—

(1) any single-family house sold or rented by an owner: Provided, That such private individual owner does not own more than three such single-family houses at any one time: Provided further, That in the case of the sale of any such single-family house by a private individual owner not residing in such house at the time of such sale or who was not the most recent resident of such house prior to such sale, the exemption granted by this subsection shall apply only with respect to one such sale within any twenty-four month period: Provided further, That such bona fide private individual owner does not own any interest in, nor is there owned or reserved on his behalf, under any express or voluntary agreement, title to or any right to all or a portion of the proceeds from the sale or rental of, more than three such single-family houses at any one time: Provided further, That after December 31, 1969, the sale or rental of any such single-family house shall be excepted from the application of this subchapter only if such house is sold or rented (A) without the use in any manner of the sales or rental facilities or the sales or rental services of any real estate broker, agent, or salesman, or of such facilities or services of any person in the business of selling or renting dwellings, or of any employee or agent of any such broker, agent, salesman, or person and (B) without the publication, posting or mailing, after notice, of any advertisement or written notice in violation of section 804(c) of this title; but nothing in this proviso shall prohibit the use of attorneys, escrow agents, abstractors, title companies, and other such professional assistance as necessary to perfect or transfer the title, or

(2) rooms or units in dwellings containing living quarters occupied or intended to be occupied by no more than four families living independently of each other, if the owner actually maintains and occupies one of such living quarters as his residence.

(c) or the purposes of subsection (b) of this section, a person shall be deemed to be in the business of selling or renting dwellings if—

(1) he has, within the preceding twelve months, participated as principal in three or more transactions involving the sale or rental of any dwelling or any interest therein, or

(2) he has, within the preceding twelve months, participated as agent, other than in the sale of his own personal residence in providing sales or rental facilities or sales or rental services in two or more transactions involving the sale or rental of any dwelling or any interest therein, or

(3) he is the owner of any dwelling designed or intended for occupancy by, or occupied by, five or more families.

SEC. 804. [42 U.S.C. 3604] DISCRIMINATION IN SALE OR RENTAL OF HOUSING AND OTHER PROHIBITED PRACTICES

As made applicable by section 803 of this title and except as exempted by sections 803(b) and 807 of this title, it shall be unlawful—

(a) To refuse to sell or rent after the making of a bona fide offer, or to refuse to negotiate for the sale or rental of, or otherwise make unavailable or deny, a dwelling to any person because of race, color, religion, sex, familial status, or national origin.

(b) To discriminate against any person in the terms, conditions, or privileges of sale or rental of a dwelling, or in the provision of services or facilities in connection therewith, because of race, color, religion, sex, familial status, or national origin.

(c) To make, print, or publish, or cause to be made, printed, or published any notice, statement, or advertisement, with respect to the sale or rental of a dwelling that indicates any preference, limitation, or discrimination based on race, color, religion, sex, handicap, familial status, or national origin, or an intention to make any such preference, limitation, or discrimination.

(d) To represent to any person because of race, color, religion, sex, handicap, familial status, or national origin that any dwelling is not available for inspection, sale, or rental when such dwelling is in fact so available.

(e) For profit, to induce or attempt to induce any person to sell or rent any dwelling by representations regarding the entry or prospective entry into the neighborhood of a person or persons of a particular race, color, religion, sex, handicap, familial status, or national origin.

(f) (1) To discriminate in the sale or rental, or to otherwise make unavailable or deny, a dwelling to any buyer or renter because of a handicap of—

(A) that buyer or renter,

(B) a person residing in or intending to reside in that dwelling after it is so sold, rented, or made available; or

(C) any person associated with that buyer or renter.

(2) To discriminate against any person in the terms, conditions, or privileges of sale or rental of a dwelling, or in the provision of ser-

vices or facilities in connection with such dwelling, because of a handicap of—

(A) that person; or

(B) a person residing in or intending to reside in that dwelling after it is so sold, rented, or made available; or

(C) any person associated with that person.

(3) For purposes of this subsection, discrimination includes—

(A) a refusal to permit, at the expense of the handicapped person, reasonable modifications of existing premises occupied or to be occupied by such person if such modifications may be necessary to afford such person full enjoyment of the premises, except that, in the case of a rental, the landlord may where it is reasonable to do so condition permission for a modification on the renter agreeing to restore the interior of the premises to the condition that existed before the modification, reasonable wear and tear excepted.

(B) a refusal to make reasonable accommodations in rules, policies, practices, or services, when such accommodations may be necessary to afford such person equal opportunity to use and enjoy a dwelling; or

(C) in connection with the design and construction of covered multifamily dwellings for first occupancy after the date that is 30 months after the date of enactment of the Fair Housing Amendments Act of 1988, a failure to design and construct those dwelling in such a manner that—

(i) the public use and common use portions of such dwellings are readily accessible to and usable by handicapped persons;

(ii) all the doors designed to allow passage into and within all premises within such dwellings are sufficiently wide to allow passage by handicapped persons in wheelchairs; and

(iii) all premises within such dwellings contain the following features of adaptive design:

(I) an accessible route into and through the dwelling;

(II) light switches, electrical outlets, thermostats, and other environmental controls in accessible locations;

(III) reinforcements in bathroom walls to allow later installation of grab bars; and

(IV) usable kitchens and bathrooms such that an individual in a wheelchair can maneuver about the space.

(4) Compliance with the appropriate requirements of the American National Standard for buildings and facilities providing accessibility and usability for physically handicapped people (commonly cited as "ANSI A117.1") suffices to satisfy the requirements of paragraph (3)(C)(iii).

(5)(A) If a State or unit of general local government has incorporated into its laws the requirements set forth in paragraph (3)(C), compliance with such laws shall be deemed to satisfy the requirements of that paragraph.

(B) A State or unit of general local government may review and approve newly constructed covered multifamily dwellings for the purpose of making determinations as to whether the design and construction requirements of paragraph (3)(C) are met.

(C) The Secretary shall encourage, but may not require, States and units of local government to include in their existing procedures for the review and approval of newly constructed covered multifamily dwellings, determinations as to whether the design and construction of such dwellings are consistent with paragraph (3)(C), and shall provide technical assistance to States and units of local government and other persons to implement the requirements of paragraph (3)(C).

(D) Nothing in this title shall be construed to require the Secretary to review or approve the plans, designs or construction of all covered multifamily dwellings, to determine whether the design and construction of such dwellings are consistent with the requirements of paragraph 3(C).

(6)(A) Nothing in paragraph (5) shall be construed to affect the authority and responsibility of the Secretary or a State or local public agency certified pursuant to section 810(f)(3) of this Act to receive and process complaints or otherwise engage in enforcement activities under this title.

(B) Determinations by a State or a unit of general local government under paragraphs (5)(A) and (B) shall not be conclusive in enforcement proceedings under this title.

(7) As used in this subsection, the term "covered multifamily dwellings" means—

(A) buildings consisting of 4 or more units if such buildings have one or more elevators; and

(B) ground floor units in other buildings consisting of 4 or more units.

(8) Nothing in this title shall be construed to invalidate or limit any law of a State or political subdivision of a State, or other jurisdiction in which this title shall be effective, that requires dwellings to be designed and constructed in a manner that affords handicapped persons greater access than is required by this title.

(9) Nothing in this subsection requires that a dwelling be made available to an individual whose tenancy would constitute a direct threat to the health or safety of other individuals or whose tenancy would result in substantial physical damage to the property of others.

SEC. 805. [42 U.S.C. 3605] DISCRIMINATION IN RESIDENTIAL REAL ESTATE-RELATED TRANSACTIONS

(a) In General.—

It shall be unlawful for any person or other entity whose business includes engaging in residential real estate-related transactions to discriminate against any person in making available such a transaction, or in the terms or conditions of such a transaction, because of race, color, religion, sex, handicap, familial status, or national origin.

(b) Definition.—

As used in this section, the term "residential real estate-related transaction" means any of the following:

(1) The making or purchasing of loans or providing other financial assistance—

(A) for purchasing, constructing, improving, repairing, or maintaining a dwelling; or

(B) secured by residential real estate.

(2) The selling, brokering, or appraising of residential real property.

(c) Appraisal Exemption.—

Nothing in this title prohibits a person engaged in the business of furnishing appraisals of real property to take into consideration factors other than race, color, religion, national origin, sex, handicap, or familial status.

SEC. 806. [42 U.S.C. 3606] DISCRIMINATION IN PROVISION OF BROKERAGE SERVICES

After December 31, 1968, it shall be unlawful to deny any person access to or membership or participation in any multiple-listing service, real estate brokers' organization or other service, organization, or facility relating to the business of selling or renting dwellings, or to discriminate against him in the terms or conditions of such access, membership, or participation, on account of race, color, religion, sex, handicap, familial status, or national origin.

SEC. 807. [42 U.S.C. 3607] RELIGIOUS ORGANIZATION OR PRIVATE CLUB EXEMPTION

(a) Nothing in this subchapter shall prohibit a religious organization, association, or society, or any nonprofit institution or organization operated, supervised or controlled by or in conjunction with a religious organization, association, or society, from limiting the sale, rental or occupancy of dwellings which it owns or operates for other than a commercial purpose to persons of the same religion, or from giving preference to such persons, unless membership in such religion is restricted on account of race, color, or national origin. Nor shall anything in this subchapter prohibit a private club not in fact open to the public, which as an incident to its primary purpose or purposes provides lodgings which it owns or operates for other than a commercial purpose, from limiting the rental or occupancy of such lodgings to its members or from giving preference to its members.

(b)(1) Nothing in this title limits the applicability of any reasonable local, State, or Federal restrictions regarding the maximum number of occupants permitted to occupy a dwelling. Nor does any provision in this title regarding familial status apply with respect to housing for older persons.

(2) As used in this section "housing for older persons" means housing—

(A) provided under any State or Federal program that the Secretary determines is specifically designed and operated to assist elderly persons (as defined in the State or Federal program); or

(B) intended for, and solely occupied by, persons 62 years of age or older; or

(C) intended and operated for occupancy by persons 55 years of age or older, and—

(i) at least 80 percent of the occupied units are occupied by at least one person who is 55 years of age or older;

(ii) the housing facility or community publishes and adheres to policies and procedures that demonstrate the intent required under this subparagraph; and

(iii) the housing facility or community complies with rules issued by the Secretary for verification of occupancy, which shall—

(I) provide for verification by reliable surveys and affidavits; and

(II) include examples of the types of policies and procedures relevant to a determination of compliance with the requirement of clause (ii). Such surveys and affidavits shall be admissible in administrative and judicial proceedings for the purposes of such verification.

(3) Housing shall not fail to meet the requirements for housing for older persons by reason of:

(A) persons residing in such housing as of the date of enactment of this Act who do not meet the age requirements of subsections (2)(B) or (C): Provided, That new occupants of such housing meet the age requirements of sections (2)(B) or (C); or

(B) unoccupied units: Provided, That such units are reserved for occupancy by persons who meet the age requirements of subsections (2)(B) or (C).

(4) Nothing in this title prohibits conduct against a person because such person has been convicted by any court of competent jurisdiction of the illegal manufacture or distribution of a controlled substance as defined in section 102 of the Controlled Substances Act (21 U.S.C. 802).

(5)(A) A person shall not be held personally liable for monetary damages for a violation of this title if such person reasonably relied, in good faith, on the application of the exemption under this subsection relating to housing for older persons.

(B) For the purposes of this paragraph, a person may only show good faith reliance on the application of the exemption by showing that—

(i) such person has no actual knowledge that the facility or community is not, or will not be, eligible for such exemption; and

(ii) the facility or community has stated formally, in writing, that the facility or community complies with the requirements for such exemption.

SEC. 808. [42 U.S.C. 3608] ADMINISTRATION

(a) Authority and responsibility

The authority and responsibility for administering this Act shall be in the Secretary of Housing and Urban Development.

(b) Assistant Secretary

The Department of Housing and Urban Development shall be provided an additional Assistant Secretary.

(c) Delegation of authority; appointment of administrative law judges; location of conciliation meetings; administrative review

The Secretary may delegate any of his functions, duties and power to employees of the Department of Housing and Urban Development or to boards of such employees, including functions, duties, and powers with respect to investigating, conciliating, hearing, determining, ordering, certifying, reporting, or otherwise acting as to any work, business, or matter under this subchapter. The person to whom such delegations are made with respect to hearing functions, duties, and powers shall be appointed and shall serve in the Department of Housing and Urban Development in compliance with sections 3105, 3344, 5372, and 7521 of title 5 [of the United States Code]. Insofar as possible, conciliation meetings shall be held in the cities or other localities where the discriminatory housing practices allegedly occurred. The Secretary shall by rule prescribe such rights of appeal from the decisions of his administrative law judges to other administrative law judges or to other officers in the Department, to boards of officers or to himself, as shall be appropriate and in accordance with law.

(d) Cooperation of Secretary and executive departments and agencies in administration of housing and urban development programs and activities to further fair housing purposes

All executive departments and agencies shall administer their programs and activities relating to housing and urban development (including any Federal agency having regulatory or supervisory authority over financial institutions) in a manner affirmatively to further the purposes of this subchapter and shall cooperate with the Secretary to further such purposes.

(e) Functions of Secretary

The Secretary of Housing and Urban Development shall—

(1) make studies with respect to the nature and extent of discriminatory housing practices in representative communities, urban, suburban, and rural, throughout the United States;

(2) publish and disseminate reports, recommendations, and information derived from such studies, including an annual report to the Congress—

(A) specifying the nature and extent of progress made nationally in eliminating discriminatory housing practices and furthering the purposes of this title, obstacles remaining to achieving equal housing opportunity, and recommendations for further legislative or executive action; and

(B) containing tabulations of the number of instances (and the reasons therefor) in the preceding year in which—

(i) investigations are not completed as required by section 810(a)(1)(B);

(ii) determinations are not made within the time specified in section 810(g); and

(iii) hearings are not commenced or findings and conclusions are not made as required by section 812(g);

(3) cooperate with and render technical assistance to Federal, State, local, and other public or private agencies, organizations, and institutions which are formulating or carrying on programs to prevent or eliminate discriminatory housing practices;

(4) cooperate with and render such technical and other assistance to the Community Relations Service as may be appropriate to further its activities in preventing or eliminating discriminatory housing practices;

(5) administer the programs and activities relating to housing and urban development in a manner affirmatively to further the policies of this subchapter; and

(6) annually report to the Congress, and make available to the public, data on the race, color, religion, sex, national origin, age, handicap, and family characteristics of persons and households who are applicants for, participants in, or beneficiaries or potential beneficiaries of, programs administered by the Department to the extent such characteristics are within the coverage of the provisions of law and Executive orders referred to in subsection (f) which apply to such programs (and in order to develop the data to be included and made available to the public under this subsection, the Secretary shall, without regard to any other provision of law, collect such information relating to those characteristics as the Secretary determines to be necessary or appropriate).

(f) The provisions of law and Executive orders to which subsection (e)(6) applies are—

(1) title VI of the Civil Rights Act of 1964;

(2) title VIII of the Civil Rights Act of 1968;

(3) section 504 of the Rehabilitation Act of 1973;

(4) the Age Discrimination Act of 1975;

(5) the Equal Credit Opportunity Act;

(6) section 1978 of the Revised Statutes (42 U.S.C. 1982);

(7) section 8(a) of the Small Business Act;

(8) section 527 of the National Housing Act;

(9) section 109 of the Housing and Community Development Act of 1974;

(10) section 3 of the Housing and Urban Development Act of 1968;

(11) Executive Orders 11063, 11246, 11625, 12250, 12259, and 12432; and

(12) any other provision of law which the Secretary specifies by publication in the Federal Register for the purpose of this subsection.

SEC. 808A. [42 U.S.C. 3608A] COLLECTION OF CERTAIN DATA

(a) In general

To assess the extent of compliance with Federal fair housing requirements (including the requirements established under title VI of Public Law 88-352 [42 U.S.C.A. {2000d et seq.] and title VIII of Public Law 90-284 [42 U.S.C.A. {3601 et seq.]), the Secretary of Housing and Urban Development and the Secretary of Agriculture shall each collect, not less than annually, data on the racial and ethnic characteristics of persons eligible for, assisted, or otherwise benefiting under each community development, housing assistance, and mortgage and loan insurance and guarantee program administered by such Secretary. Such data shall be collected on a building by building basis if the Secretary involved determines such collection to be appropriate.

(b) Reports to Congress

The Secretary of Housing and Urban Development and the Secretary of Agriculture shall each include in the annual report of such Secretary to the Congress a summary and evaluation of the data collected by such Secretary under subsection (a) of this section during the preceding year.

SEC. 809. [42 U.S.C. 3609] EDUCATION AND CONCILIATION; CONFERENCES AND CONSULTATIONS; REPORTS

Immediately after April 11, 1968, the Secretary shall commence such educational and conciliatory activities as in his judgment will further the purposes of this subchapter. He shall call conferences of persons in the housing industry and other interested parties to acquaint them with the provisions of this subchapter and his suggested means of implementing it, and shall endeavor with their advice to work out programs of voluntary compliance and of enforcement. He may pay per diem, travel, and transportation expenses for persons attending such conferences as provided in section 5703 of Title 5. He shall consult with State and local officials and other interested parties to learn the extent, if any, to which housing discrimination exists in their State or locality, and whether and how State or local enforcement programs might be utilized to combat such discrimination in connection with or in place of, the Secretary's enforcement of this subchapter. The Secretary shall issue reports on such conferences and consultations as he deems appropriate.

SEC. 810. [42 U.S.C. 3610] ADMINISTRATIVE ENFORCEMENT; PRELIMINARY MATTERS

(a) Complaints and Answers.—

(1) (A) (i) An aggrieved person may, not later than one year after an alleged discriminatory housing practice has occurred or terminated, file a complaint with the Secretary alleging such discriminatory housing practice. The Secretary, on the Secretary's own initiative, may also file such a complaint.

(ii) Such complaints shall be in writing and shall contain such information and be in such form as the Secretary requires.

(iii) The Secretary may also investigate housing practices to determine whether a complaint should be brought under this section.

(B) Upon the filing of such a complaint—

(i) the Secretary shall serve notice upon the aggrieved person acknowledging such filing and advising the aggrieved person of the time limits and choice of forums provided under this title;

(ii) the Secretary shall, not later than 10 days after such filing or the identification of an additional respondent under paragraph (2), serve on the respondent a notice identifying the alleged discriminatory housing practice and advising such respondent of the procedural rights and obligations of respondents under this title, together with a copy of the original complaint;

(iii) each respondent may file, not later than 10 days after receipt of notice from the Secretary, an answer to such complaint; and

(iv) the Secretary shall make an investigation of the alleged discriminatory housing practice and complete such investigation within 100 days after the filing of the complaint (or, when the Secretary takes further action under subsection (f)(2) with respect to a complaint, within 100 days after the commencement of such further action), unless it is impracticable to do so.

(C) If the Secretary is unable to complete the investigation within 100 days after the filing of the complaint (or, when the Secretary takes further action under subsection (f)(2) with respect to a complaint, within 100 days after the commencement of such further action), the Secretary shall notify the complainant and respondent in writing of the reasons for not doing so.

(D) Complaints and answers shall be under oath or affirmation, and may be reasonably and fairly amended at any time.

(2)(A) A person who is not named as a respondent in a complaint, but who is identified as a respondent in the course of investigation, may be joined as an additional or substitute respondent upon written notice, under paragraph (1), to such person, from the Secretary.

(B) Such notice, in addition to meeting the requirements of paragraph (1), shall explain the basis for the Secretary's belief that the person to whom the notice is addressed is properly joined as a respondent.

(b) Investigative Report and Conciliation.—

(1) During the period beginning with the filing of such complaint and ending with the filing of a charge or a dismissal by the Secretary, the Secretary shall, to the extent feasible, engage in conciliation with respect to such complaint.

(2) A conciliation agreement arising out of such conciliation shall be an agreement between the respondent and the complainant, and shall be subject to approval by the Secretary.

(3) A conciliation agreement may provide for binding arbitration of the dispute arising from the complaint. Any such arbitration that results from a conciliation agreement may award appropriate relief, including monetary relief.

(4) Each conciliation agreement shall be made public unless the complainant and respondent otherwise agree and the Secretary determines that disclosure is not required to further the purposes of this title.

(5)(A) At the end of each investigation under this section, the Secretary shall prepare a final investigative report containing—

(i) the names and dates of contacts with witnesses;

(ii) a summary and the dates of correspondence and other contacts with the aggrieved person and the respondent;

(iii) a summary description of other pertinent records;

(iv) a summary of witness statements; and

(v) answers to interrogatories.

(B) A final report under this paragraph may be amended if additional evidence is later discovered.

(c) Failure to Comply With Conciliation Agreement.—

Whenever the Secretary has reasonable cause to believe that a respondent has breached a conciliation agreement, the Secretary shall refer the matter to the Attorney General with a recommendation that a civil action be filed under section 814 for the enforcement of such agreement.

(d) Prohibitions and Requirements With Respect to Disclosure of Information.—

(1) Nothing said or done in the course of conciliation under this title may be made public or used as evidence in a subsequent proceeding under this title without the written consent of the persons concerned.

(2) Notwithstanding paragraph (1), the Secretary shall make available to the aggrieved person and the respondent, at any time, upon request following completion of the Secretary's investigation, information derived from an investigation and any final investigative report relating to that investigation.

(e) Prompt Judicial Action.—

(1) If the Secretary concludes at any time following the filing of a complaint that prompt judicial action is necessary to carry out the purposes of this title, the Secretary may authorize a civil action for appropriate temporary or preliminary relief pending final disposition of the complaint under this section. Upon receipt of such authorization, the Attorney General shall promptly commence and maintain such an action. Any temporary restraining order or other order granting preliminary or temporary relief shall be issued in accordance with the Federal Rules of Civil Procedure. The commencement of a civil action under this subsection does not affect the initiation or continuation of administrative proceedings under this section and section 812 of this title.

(2) Whenever the Secretary has reason to believe that a basis may exist for the commencement of proceedings against any respondent under section 814(a) and 814(c) or for proceedings by any governmental licensing or supervisory authorities, the Secretary shall transmit the in-

formation upon which such belief is based to the Attorney General, or to such authorities, as the case may be.

(f) Referral for State or Local Proceedings.—

(1) Whenever a complaint alleges a discriminatory housing practice—

(A) within the jurisdiction of a State or local public agency; and

(B) as to which such agency has been certified by the Secretary under this subsection; the Secretary shall refer such complaint to that certified agency before taking any action with respect to such complaint.

(2) Except with the consent of such certified agency, the Secretary, after that referral is made, shall take no further action with respect to such complaint unless—

(A) the certified agency has failed to commence proceedings with respect to the complaint before the end of the 30th day after the date of such referral;

(B) the certified agency, having so commenced such proceedings, fails to carry forward such proceedings with reasonable promptness; or

(C) the Secretary determines that the certified agency no longer qualifies for certification under this subsection with respect to the relevant jurisdiction.

(3)(A) The Secretary may certify an agency under this subsection only if the Secretary determines that—

(i) the substantive rights protected by such agency in the jurisdiction with respect to which certification is to be made;

(ii) the procedures followed by such agency;

(iii) the remedies available to such agency; and

(iv) the availability of judicial review of such agency's action;

are substantially equivalent to those created by and under this title.

(B) Before making such certification, the Secretary shall take into account the current practices and past performance, if any, of such agency.

(4) During the period which begins on the date of the enactment of the Fair Housing Amendments Act of 1988 and ends 40 months after such date, each agency certified (including an agency certified for interim referrals pursuant to 24 CFR 115.11, unless such agency is subsequently denied recognition under 24 CFR 115.7) for the purposes of this title on the day before such date shall for the purposes of this sub-

section be considered certified under this subsection with respect to those matters for which such agency was certified on that date. If the Secretary determines in an individual case that an agency has not been able to meet the certification requirements within this 40-month period due to exceptional circumstances, such as the infrequency of legislative sessions in that jurisdiction, the Secretary may extend such period by not more than 8 months.

(5) Not less frequently than every 5 years, the Secretary shall determine whether each agency certified under this subsection continues to qualify for certification. The Secretary shall take appropriate action with respect to any agency not so qualifying.

(g) Reasonable Cause Determination and Effect.—

(1) The Secretary shall, within 100 days after the filing of the complaint (or, when the Secretary takes further action under subsection (f)(2) with respect to a complaint, within 100 days after the commencement of such further action), determine based on the facts whether reasonable cause exists to believe that a discriminatory housing practice has occurred or is about to occur, unless it is impracticable to do so, or unless the Secretary has approved a conciliation agreement with respect to the complaint. If the Secretary is unable to make the determination within 100 days after the filing of the complaint (or, when the Secretary takes further action under subsection (f)(2) with respect to a complaint, within 100 days after the commencement of such further action), the Secretary shall notify the complainant and respondent in writing of the reasons for not doing so.

(2)(A) If the Secretary determines that reasonable cause exists to believe that a discriminatory housing practice has occurred or is about to occur, the Secretary shall, except as provided in subparagraph (C), immediately issue a charge on behalf of the aggrieved person, for further proceedings under section 812.

(B) Such charge—

(i) shall consist of a short and plain statement of the facts upon which the Secretary has found reasonable cause to believe that a discriminatory housing practice has occurred or is about to occur;

(ii) shall be based on the final investigative report; and

(iii) need not be limited to the facts or grounds alleged in the complaint filed under section 810(a).

(C) If the Secretary determines that the matter involves the legality of any State or local zoning or other land use law or ordinance, the Secretary shall immediately refer the matter to the Attorney General for appropriate action under section 814, instead of issuing such charge.

(3) If the Secretary determines that no reasonable cause exists to believe that a discriminatory housing practice has occurred or is about to occur, the Secretary shall promptly dismiss the complaint. The Secretary shall make public disclosure of each such dismissal.

(4) The Secretary may not issue a charge under this section regarding an alleged discriminatory housing practice after the beginning of the trial of a civil action commenced by the aggrieved party under an Act of Congress or a State law, seeking relief with respect to that discriminatory housing practice.

(h) Service of Copies of Charge.—

After the Secretary issues a charge under this section, the Secretary shall cause a copy thereof, together with information as to how to make an election under section 812(a) and the effect of such an election, to be served—

(1) on each respondent named in such charge, together with a notice of opportunity for a hearing at a time and place specified in the notice, unless that election is made; and

(2) on each aggrieved person on whose behalf the complaint was filed.

SEC. 811. [42 U.S.C. 3611] SUBPOENAS; GIVING OF EVIDENCE

(a) In General.—

The Secretary may, in accordance with this subsection, issue subpoenas and order discovery in aid of investigations and hearings under this title. Such subpoenas and discovery may be ordered to the same extent and subject to the same limitations as would apply if the subpoenas or discovery were ordered or served in aid of a civil action in the United States district court for the district in which the investigation is taking place.

(b) Witness Fees.—

Witnesses summoned by a subpoena under this title shall be entitled to same witness and mileage fees as witnesses in proceedings in United States district courts. Fees payable to a witness summoned by a subpoena issued at the request of a party shall be paid by that party or, where a party is unable to pay the fees, by the Secretary.

(c) Criminal Penalties.—

(1) Any person who willfully fails or neglects to attend and testify or to answer any lawful inquiry or to produce records, documents, or other evidence, if it is in such person's power to do so, in obedience to the subpoena or other lawful order under subsection (a), shall be fined not more than $100,000 or imprisoned not more than one year, or both.

(2) Any person who, with intent thereby to mislead another person in any proceeding under this title—

(A) makes or causes to be made any false entry or statement of fact in any report, account, record, or other document produced pursuant to subpoena or other lawful order under subsection (a);

(B) willfully neglects or fails to make or to cause to be made full, true, and correct entries in such reports, accounts, records, or other documents; or

(C) willfully mutilates, alters, or by any other means falsifies any documentary evidence;

shall be fined not more than $100,000 or imprisoned not more than one year, or both.

SEC. 812. [42 U.S.C. 3612] ENFORCEMENT BY SECRETARY

(a) Election of Judicial Determination.—

When a charge is filed under section 810, a complainant, a respondent, or an aggrieved person on whose behalf the complaint was filed, may elect to have the claims asserted in that charge decided in a civil action under subsection (o) in lieu of a hearing under subsection (b). The election must be made not later than 20 days after the receipt by the electing person of service under section 810(h) or, in the case of the Secretary, not later than 20 days after such service. The person making such election shall give notice of doing so to the Secretary and to all other complainants and respondents to whom the charge relates.

(b) Administrative Law Judge Hearing in Absence of Election.—

If an election is not made under subsection (a) with respect to a charge filed under section 810, the Secretary shall provide an opportunity for a hearing on the record with respect to a charge issued under section 810. The Secretary shall delegate the conduct of a hearing under this section to an administrative law judge appointed under section 3105 of title 5, United States Code. The administrative law judge shall conduct the hearing at a place in the vicinity in which the discriminatory housing practice is alleged to have occurred or to be about to occur.

(c) Rights of Parties.—

At a hearing under this section, each party may appear in person, be represented by counsel, present evidence, cross-examine witnesses, and obtain the issuance of subpoenas under section 811. Any aggrieved person may intervene as a party in the proceeding. The Federal Rules of Evidence apply to the presentation of evidence in such hearing as they would in a civil action in a United States district court.

(d) Expedited Discovery and Hearing.—

(1) Discovery in administrative proceedings under this section shall be conducted as expeditiously and inexpensively as possible, consistent with the need of all parties to obtain relevant evidence.

(2) A hearing under this section shall be conducted as expeditiously and inexpensively as possible, consistent with the needs and rights of the parties to obtain a fair hearing and a complete record.

(3) The Secretary shall, not later than 180 days after the date of enactment of this subsection, issue rules to implement this subsection.

(e) Resolution of Charge.—

Any resolution of a charge before a final order under this section shall require the consent of the aggrieved person on whose behalf the charge is issued.

(f) Effect of Trial of Civil Action on Administrative Proceedings.—

An administrative law judge may not continue administrative proceedings under this section regarding any alleged discriminatory housing practice after the beginning of the trial of a civil action commenced by the aggrieved party under an Act of Congress or a State law, seeking relief with respect to that discriminatory housing practice.

(g) Hearings, Findings and Conclusions, and Order.—

(1) The administrative law judge shall commence the hearing under this section no later than 120 days following the issuance of the charge, unless it is impracticable to do so. If the administrative law judge is unable to commence the hearing within 120 days after the issuance of the charge, the administrative law judge shall notify the Secretary, the aggrieved person on whose behalf the charge was filed, and the respondent, in writing of the reasons for not doing so.

(2) The administrative law judge shall make findings of fact and conclusions of law within 60 days after the end of the hearing under this section, unless it is impracticable to do so. If the administrative law judge is unable to make findings of fact and conclusions of law within such period, or any succeeding 60-day period thereafter, the adminis-

trative law judge shall notify the Secretary, the aggrieved person on whose behalf the charge was filed, and the respondent, in writing of the reasons for not doing so.

(3) If the administrative law judge finds that a respondent has engaged or is about to engage in a discriminatory housing practice, such administrative law judge shall promptly issue an order for such relief as may be appropriate, which may include actual damages suffered by the aggrieved person and injunctive or other equitable relief. Such order may, to vindicate the public interest, assess a civil penalty against the respondent—

(A) in an amount not exceeding $11,000 if the respondent has not been adjudged to have committed any prior discriminatory housing practice;

(B) in an amount not exceeding $27,500 if the respondent has been adjudged to have committed one other discriminatory housing practice during the 5-year period ending on the date of the filing of this charge; and

(C) in an amount not exceeding $55,000 if the respondent has been adjudged to have committed 2 or more discriminatory housing practices during the 7-year period ending on the date of the filing of this charge;

except that if the acts constituting the discriminatory housing practice that is the object of the charge are committed by the same natural person who has been previously adjudged to have committed acts constituting a discriminatory housing practice, then the civil penalties set forth in subparagraphs (B) and (C) may be imposed without regard to the period of time within which any subsequent discriminatory housing practice occurred.

(4) No such order shall affect any contract, sale, encumbrance, or lease consummated before the issuance of such order and involving a bona fide purchaser, encumbrancer, or tenant without actual notice of the charge filed under this title.

(5) In the case of an order with respect to a discriminatory housing practice that occurred in the course of a business subject to a licensing or regulation by a governmental agency, the Secretary shall, not later than 30 days after the date of the issuance of such order (or, if such order is judicially reviewed, 30 days after such order is in substance affirmed upon such review)—

(A) send copies of the findings of fact, conclusions of law, and the order, to that governmental agency; and

(B) recommend to that governmental agency appropriate disciplinary action (including, where appropriate, the suspension or revocation of the license of the respondent).

(6) In the case of an order against a respondent against whom another order was issued within the preceding 5 years under this section, the Secretary shall send a copy of each such order to the Attorney General.

(7) If the administrative law judge finds that the respondent has not engaged or is not about to engage in a discriminatory housing practice, as the case may be, such administrative law judge shall enter an order dismissing the charge. The Secretary shall make public disclosure of each such dismissal.

(h) Review by Secretary; Service of Final Order.—

(1) The Secretary may review any finding, conclusion, or order issued under subsection (g). Such review shall be completed not later than 30 days after the finding, conclusion, or order is so issued; otherwise the finding, conclusion, or order becomes final.

(2) The Secretary shall cause the findings of fact and conclusions of law made with respect to any final order for relief under this section, together with a copy of such order, to be served on each aggrieved person and each respondent in the proceeding.

(i) Judicial Review.—

(1) Any party aggrieved by a final order for relief under this section granting or denying in whole or in part the relief sought may obtain a review of such order under chapter 158 of title 28, United States Code.

(2) Notwithstanding such chapter, venue of the proceeding shall be in the judicial circuit in which the discriminatory housing practice is alleged to have occurred, and filing of the petition for review shall be not later than 30 days after the order is entered.

(j) Court Enforcement of Administrative Order Upon Petition by Secretary.—

(1) The Secretary may petition any United States court of appeals for the circuit in which the discriminatory housing practice is alleged to have occurred or in which any respondent resides or transacts business for the enforcement of the order of the administrative law judge and for appropriate temporary relief or restraining order, by filing in such court a written petition praying that such order be enforced and for appropriate temporary relief or restraining order.

(2) The Secretary shall file in court with the petition the record in the proceeding. A copy of such petition shall be forthwith transmitted by

the clerk of the court to the parties to the proceeding before the administrative law judge.

(k) Relief Which May Be Granted.—

(1) Upon the filing of a petition under subsection (i) or (j), the court may—

(A) grant to the petitioner, or any other party, such temporary relief, restraining order, or other order as the court deems just and proper;

(B) affirm, modify, or set aside, in whole or in part, the order, or remand the order for further proceedings; and

(C) enforce such order to the extent that such order is affirmed or modified.

(2) Any party to the proceeding before the administrative law judge may intervene in the court of appeals.

(3) No objection not made before the administrative law judge shall be considered by the court, unless the failure or neglect to urge such objection is excused because of extraordinary circumstances.

(l) Enforcement Decree in Absence of Petition for Review.—

If no petition for review is filed under subsection (i) before the expiration of 45 days after the date the administrative law judge's order is entered, the administrative law judge's findings of fact and order shall be conclusive in connection with any petition for enforcement—

(1) which is filed by the Secretary under subsection (j) after the end of such day; or

(2) under subsection (m).

(m) Court Enforcement of Administrative Order Upon Petition of Any Person Entitled to Relief.—

If before the expiration of 60 days after the date the administrative law judge's order is entered, no petition for review has been filed under subsection (i), and the Secretary has not sought enforcement of the order under subsection (j), any person entitled to relief under the order may petition for a decree enforcing the order in the United States court of appeals for the circuit in which the discriminatory housing practice is alleged to have occurred.

(n) Entry of Decree.—

The clerk of the court of appeals in which a petition for enforcement is filed under subsection (1) or (m) shall forthwith enter a decree enforcing the order and shall transmit a copy of such decree to the Secretary, the respondent named in the petition, and to any other parties to the proceeding before the administrative law judge.

(o) Civil Action for Enforcement When Election Is Made for Such Civil Action.—

(1) If an election is made under subsection (a), the Secretary shall authorize, and not later than 30 days after the election is made the Attorney General shall commence and maintain, a civil action on behalf of the aggrieved person in a United States district court seeking relief under this subsection. Venue for such civil action shall be determined under chapter 87 of title 28, United States Code.

(2) Any aggrieved person with respect to the issues to be determined in a civil action under this subsection may intervene as of right in that civil action.

(3) In a civil action under this subsection, if the court finds that a discriminatory housing practice has occurred or is about to occur, the court may grant as relief any relief which a court could grant with respect to such discriminatory housing practice in a civil action under section 813. Any relief so granted that would accrue to an aggrieved person in a civil action commenced by that aggrieved person under section 813 shall also accrue to that aggrieved person in a civil action under this subsection. If monetary relief is sought for the benefit of an aggrieved person who does not intervene in the civil action, the court shall not award such relief if that aggrieved person has not complied with discovery orders entered by the court.

(p) Attorney's Fees.—

In any administrative proceeding brought under this section, or any court proceeding arising therefrom, or any civil action under section 812, the administrative law judge or the court, as the case may be, in its discretion, may allow the prevailing party, other than the United States, a reasonable attorney's fee and costs. The United States shall be liable for such fees and costs to the extent provided by section 504 of title 5, United States Code, or by section 2412 of title 28, United States Code.

SEC. 813. [42 U.S.C. 3613] ENFORCEMENT BY PRIVATE PERSONS

(a) Civil Action.—

(1)(A) An aggrieved person may commence a civil action in an appropriate United States district court or State court not later than 2 years after the occurrence or the termination of an alleged discriminatory housing practice, or the breach of a conciliation agreement entered into under this title, whichever occurs last, to obtain appropriate relief with respect to such discriminatory housing practice or breach.

(B) The computation of such 2-year period shall not include any time during which an administrative proceeding under this title was pending with respect to a complaint or charge under this title based upon such discriminatory housing practice. This subparagraph does not apply to actions arising from a breach of a conciliation agreement.

(2) An aggrieved person may commence a civil action under this subsection whether or not a complaint has been filed under section 810(a) and without regard to the status of any such complaint, but if the Secretary or a State or local agency has obtained a conciliation agreement with the consent of an aggrieved person, no action may be filed under this subsection by such aggrieved person with respect to the alleged discriminatory housing practice which forms the basis for such complaint except for the purpose of enforcing the terms of such an agreement.

(3) An aggrieved person may not commence a civil action under this subsection with respect to an alleged discriminatory housing practice which forms the basis of a charge issued by the Secretary if an administrative law judge has commenced a hearing on the record under this title with respect to such charge.

(b) Appointment of Attorney by Court.—

Upon application by a person alleging a discriminatory housing practice or a person against whom such a practice is alleged, the court may—

(1) appoint an attorney for such person; or

(2) authorize the commencement or continuation of a civil action under subsection (a) without the payment of fees, costs, or security, if in the opinion of the court such person is financially unable to bear the costs of such action.

(c) Relief Which May Be Granted.—

(1) In a civil action under subsection (a), if the court finds that a discriminatory housing practice has occurred or is about to occur, the court may award to the plaintiff actual and punitive damages, and subject to subsection (d), may grant as relief, as the court deems appropriate, any permanent or temporary injunction, temporary restraining order, or other order (including an order enjoining the defendant from engaging in such practice or ordering such affirmative action as may be appropriate).

(2) In a civil action under subsection (a), the court, in its discretion, may allow the prevailing party, other than the United States, a reasonable attorney's fee and costs. The United States shall be liable for such fees and costs to the same extent as a private person.

(d) Effect on Certain Sales, Encumbrances, and Rentals.—

Relief granted under this section shall not affect any contract, sale, encumbrance, or lease consummated before the granting of such relief and involving a bona fide purchaser, encumbrancer, or tenant, without actual notice of the filing of a complaint with the Secretary or civil action under this title.

(e) Intervention by Attorney General.—

Upon timely application, the Attorney General may intervene in such civil action, if the Attorney General certifies that the case is of general public importance. Upon such intervention the Attorney General may obtain such relief as would be available to the Attorney General under section 814(e) in a civil action to which such section applies.

SEC. 814. [42 U.S.C. 3614] ENFORCEMENT BY THE ATTORNEY GENERAL

(a) Pattern or Practice Cases.—

Whenever the Attorney General has reasonable cause to believe that any person or group of persons is engaged in a pattern or practice of resistance to the full enjoyment of any of the rights granted by this title, or that any group of persons has been denied any of the rights granted by this title and such denial raises an issue of general public importance, the Attorney General may commence a civil action in any appropriate United States district court.

(b) On Referral of Discriminatory Housing Practice or Conciliation Agreement for Enforcement.—

(1)(A) The Attorney General may commence a civil action in any appropriate United States district court for appropriate relief with respect to a discriminatory housing practice referred to the Attorney General by the Secretary under section 810(g).

(B) A civil action under this paragraph may be commenced not later than the expiration of 18 months after the date of the occurrence or the termination of the alleged discriminatory housing practice.

(2)(A) The Attorney General may commence a civil action in any appropriate United States district court for appropriate relief with respect to breach of a conciliation agreement referred to the Attorney General by the Secretary under section 810(c).

(B) A civil action may be commenced under this paragraph not later than the expiration of 90 days after the referral of the alleged breach under section 810(c).

(c) Enforcement of Subpoenas.—

The Attorney General, on behalf of the Secretary, or other party at whose request a subpoena is issued, under this title, may enforce such subpoena in appropriate proceedings in the United States district court for the district in which the person to whom the subpoena was addressed resides, was served, or transacts business.

(d) Relief Which May Be Granted in Civil Actions Under Subsections (a) and (b).—

(1) In a civil action under subsection (a) or (b), the court—

(A) may award such preventive relief, including a permanent or temporary injunction, restraining order, or other order against the person responsible for a violation of this title as is necessary to assure the full enjoyment of the rights granted by this title;

(B) may award such other relief as the court deems appropriate, including monetary damages to persons aggrieved; and

(C) may, to vindicate the public interest, assess a civil penalty against the respondent—

(i) in an amount not exceeding $55,000, for a first violation; and

(ii) in an amount not exceeding $110,000, for any subsequent violation.

(2) In a civil action under this section, the court, in its discretion, may allow the prevailing party, other than the United States, a reasonable attorney's fee and costs. The United States shall be liable for such fees and costs to the extent provided by section 2412 of title 28, United States Code.

(e) Intervention in Civil Actions.—

Upon timely application, any person may intervene in a civil action commenced by the Attorney General under subsection (a) or (b) which involves an alleged discriminatory housing practice with respect to which such person is an aggrieved person or a conciliation agreement to which such person is a party. The court may grant such appropriate relief to any such intervening party as is authorized to be granted to a plaintiff in a civil action under section 813.

SEC. 814A. INCENTIVES FOR SELF-TESTING AND SELF-CORRECTION

(a) Privileged Information.—

(1) Conditions For Privilege.— A report or result of a self-test (as that term is defined by regulation of the Secretary) shall be considered to be privileged under paragraph (2) if any person-

(A) conducts, or authorizes an independent third party to conduct, a self-test of any aspect of a residential real estate related lending transaction of that person, or any part of that transaction, in order to determine the level or effectiveness of compliance with this title by that person; and

(B) has identified any possible violation of this title by that person and has taken, or is taking, appropriate corrective action to address any such possible violation.

(2) Privileged Self-Test.— If a person meets the conditions specified in subparagraphs (A) and (B) of paragraph (1) with respect to a self-test described in that paragraph, any report or results of that self-test-

(A) shall be privileged; and

(B) may not be obtained or used by any applicant, department, or agency in any—

(i) proceeding or civil action in which one or more violations of this title are alleged; or

(ii) examination or investigation relating to compliance with this title.

(b) Results of Self-Testing.—

(1) In General.— No provision of this section may be construed to prevent an aggrieved person, complainant, department, or agency from obtaining or using a report or results of any self-test in any proceeding or civil action in which a violation of this title is alleged, or in any examination or investigation of compliance with this title if—

(A) the person to whom the self-test relates or any person with lawful access to the report or the results—

(i) voluntarily releases or discloses all, or any part of, the report or results to the aggrieved person, complainant, department, or agency, or to the general public; or

(ii) refers to or describes the report or results as a defense to charges of violations of this title against the person to whom the self-test relates; or

(B) the report or results are sought in conjunction with an adjudication or admission of a violation of this title for the sole purpose of determining an appropriate penalty or remedy.

(2) Disclosure for Determination of Penalty or Remedy.— Any report or results of a self-test that are disclosed for the purpose specified in paragraph (1)(B)—

(A) shall be used only for the particular proceeding in which the adjudication or admission referred to in paragraph (1)(B) is made; and

(B) may not be used in any other action or proceeding.

(c) Adjudication.—

An aggrieved person, complainant, department, or agency that challenges a privilege asserted under this section may seek a determination of the existence and application of that privilege in—

(1) a court of competent jurisdiction; or

(2) an administrative law proceeding with appropriate jurisdiction.

(2) Regulations.—

(A) In General.— Not later than 6 months after the date of enactment of this Act, in consultation with the Board and after providing notice and an opportunity for public comment, the Secretary of Housing and Urban Development shall prescribe final regulations to implement section 814A of the Fair Housing Act, as added by this section.

(B) Self-Test.—

(i) Definition.— The regulations prescribed by the Secretary under subparagraph (A) shall include a definition of the term "self-test" for purposes of section 814A of the Fair Housing Act, as added by this section.

(ii) Requirement for Self-Test.— The regulations prescribed by the Secretary under subparagraph (A) shall specify that a self-test shall be sufficiently extensive to constitute a determination of the level and effectiveness of the compliance by a person engaged in residential real estate related lending activities with the Fair Housing Act.

(iii) Substantial Similarity to Certain Equal Credit Opportunity Act Regulations.— The regulations prescribed under subparagraph (A) shall be substantially similar to the regulations prescribed by the Board to carry out section 704A of the Equal Credit Opportunity Act, as added by this section.

(c) Applicability.—

(1) In General.— Except as provided in paragraph (2), the privilege provided for in section 704a of the Equal Credit Opportunity Act or section 814a of the Fair Housing Act (as those sections are added by this section) shall apply to a self-test (as that term is defined pursuant to the regulations prescribed under subsection (a)(2) or (b)(2) of this section, as appropriate) conducted before, on, or after the effective date of the regulations prescribed under subsection (a)(2) or (b)(2), as appropriate.

(2) Exception.— The privilege referred to in paragraph (1) does not apply to such a self-test conducted before the effective date of the regulations prescribed under subsection (a) or (b), as appropriate, if—

(A) before that effective date, a complaint against the creditor or person engaged in residential real estate related lending activities (as the case may be) was—

(i) formally filed in any court of competent jurisdiction; or

(ii) the subject of an ongoing administrative law proceeding;

(B) in the case of section 704a of the Equal Credit Opportunity Act, the creditor has waived the privilege pursuant to subsection (b)(1)(A)(i) of that section; or

(C) in the case of section 814a of the Fair Housing Act, the person engaged in residential real estate related lending activities has waived the privilege pursuant to subsection (b)(1)(A)(i) of that section.

SEC. 815. [42 U.S.C. 3614A] RULES TO IMPLEMENT TITLE

The Secretary may make rules (including rules for the collection, maintenance, and analysis of appropriate data) to carry out this title. The Secretary shall give public notice and opportunity for comment with respect to all rules made under this section.

SEC. 816. [42 U.S.C. 3615] EFFECT ON STATE LAWS

Nothing in this subchapter shall be constructed to invalidate or limit any law of a State or political subdivision of a State, or of any other jurisdiction in which this subchapter shall be effective, that grants, guarantees, or protects the same rights as are granted by this subchapter; but any law of a State, a political subdivision, or other such jurisdiction that purports to require or permit any action that would be a discriminatory housing practice under this subchapter shall to that extent be invalid.

SEC. 817. [42 U.S.C. 3616] COOPERATION WITH STATE AND LOCAL AGENCIES ADMINISTERING FAIR HOUSING LAWS; UTILIZATION OF SERVICES AND PERSONNEL; REIMBURSEMENT; WRITTEN AGREEMENTS; PUBLICATION IN FEDERAL REGISTER

The Secretary may cooperate with State and local agencies charged with the administration of State and local fair housing laws and, with the consent of such agencies, utilize the services of such agencies and their employees and, notwithstanding any other provision of law, may reimburse such agencies and their employees for services rendered to assist him in carrying out this subchapter. In furtherance of such cooperative efforts, the Secretary may enter into written agreements with such State or local agencies. All agreements and terminations thereof shall be published in the Federal Register.

SEC. 818. [42 U.S.C. 3617] INTERFERENCE, COERCION, OR INTIMIDATION; ENFORCEMENT BY CIVIL ACTION

It shall be unlawful to coerce, intimidate, threaten, or interfere with any person in the exercise or enjoyment of, or on account of his having exercised or enjoyed, or on account of his having aided or encouraged any other person in the exercise or enjoyment of, any right granted or protected by section 803, 804, 805, or 806 of this title.

SEC. 819. [42 U.S.C. 3618] AUTHORIZATION OF APPROPRIATIONS

There are hereby authorized to be appropriated such sums as are necessary to carry out the purposes of this subchapter.

SEC. 820. [42 U.S.C. 3619] SEPARABILITY OF PROVISIONS

If any provision of this subchapter or the application thereof to any person or circumstances is held invalid, the remainder of the subchapter and the application of the provision to other persons not similarly situated or to other circumstances shall not be affected thereby.

(Sec. 12 of 1988 Act). [42 U.S.C. 3601 note] Disclaimer of Preemptive Effect on Other Acts

Nothing in the Fair Housing Act as amended by this Act limits any right, procedure, or remedy available under the Constitution or any other Act of the Congress not so amended.

(Sec. 13 of 1988 Act). [42 U.S.C. 3601 note] Effective Date and Initial Rulemaking

(a) Effective Date.—

This Act and the amendments made by this Act shall take effect on the 180th day beginning after the date of the enactment of this Act.

(b) Initial Rulemaking.—

In consultation with other appropriate Federal agencies, the Secretary shall, not later than the 180th day after the date of the enactment of this Act, issue rules to implement title VIII as amended by this Act. The Secretary shall give public notice and opportunity for comment with respect to such rules.

(Sec. 14 of 1988 Act). [42 U.S.C. 3601 note] Separability of Provisions

If any provision of this Act or the application thereof to any person or circumstances is held invalid, the remainder of the Act and the application of the provision to other persons not similarly situated or to other circumstances shall not be affected thereby.

SECTION 901. (TITLE IX AS AMENDED) [42 U.S.C. 3631] VIOLATIONS; BODILY INJURY; DEATH; PENALTIES

Whoever, whether or not acting under color of law, by force or threat of force willfully injures, intimidates or interferes with, or attempts to injure, intimidate or interfere with—

(A) any person because of his race, color, religion, sex, handicap (as such term is defined in section 802 of this Act), familial status (as such term is defined in section 802 of this Act), or national origin and because he is or has been selling, purchasing, renting, financing occupying, or contracting or negotiating for the sale, purchase, rental, financing or occupation of any dwelling, or applying for or participating in any service, organization, or facility relating to the business of selling or renting dwellings; or

(B) any person because he is or has been, or in order to intimidate such person or any other person or any class of persons from—

(1) participating, without discrimination on account of race, color, religion, sex, handicap (as such term is defined in section 802 of this Act), familial status (as such term is defined in section 802 of this Act), or national origin, in any of the activities, services, organizations or facilities described in subsection(a) of this section; or

(2) affording another person or class of persons opportunity or protection so to participate; or

(C) any citizen because he is or has been, or in order to discourage such citizen or any other citizen from lawfully aiding or encouraging other persons to participate, without discrimination on account of race, color, religion, sex, handicap (as such term is defined in section 802 of this Act), familial status (as such term is defined in section 802 of this Act), or national origin, in any of the activities, services, organizations or facilities described in subsection (a) of this section, or participating lawfully in speech or peaceful assembly opposing any denial of the opportunity to so participate—

shall be fined not more than $1,000, or imprisoned not more than one year, or both; and if bodily injury results shall be fined not more than $10,000, or imprisoned not more than ten years, or both; and if death results shall be subject to imprisonment for any term of years or for life.

TITLE 28, UNITED STATES CODE, AS AMENDED

Section 2341. Definitions

As used in this chapter—

(1) "clerk" means the clerk of the court in which the petition for the review of an order, reviewable under this chapter, is filed;

(2) "petitioner" means the party or parties by whom a petition to review an order, reviewable under this chapter, is filed; and

(3) "agency" means—

(A) the Commission, when the order sought to be reviewed was entered by the Federal Communications Commission, the Federal Maritime Commission, the Interstate Commerce Commission, or the Atomic Energy Commission, as the case may be;

(B) the Secretary, when the order was entered by the Secretary of Agriculture;

(C) the Administration, when the order was entered by the Maritime Administration; and

(D) the Secretary, when the order is under section 812 of the Fair Housing Act.

Section 2342. Jurisdiction of court of appeals

The court of appeals (other than the United States Court of Appeals for the Federal Circuit) has exclusive jurisdiction to enjoin, set aside, suspend (in whole or in part), or to determine the validity of—

(1) all final orders of the Federal Communications Commission made reviewable by section 402(a) of title 47;

(2) all final orders of the Secretary of Agriculture made under chapters 9 and 20A of title 7, except orders issued under section 210(e), 217a, and 499g(a) of title 7;

(3) all rules, regulations, or final orders of-

(A) the Secretary of Transportation issued pursuant to section 2, 9, 37, 41, or 43 of the Shipping Act, 1916 (46 U.S.C.App. 802, 803, 808, 835, 839, and 841(a); and

(B) the Federal Maritime Commission issued pursuant to—

(i) section 23, 25, or 43 of the Shipping Act, 1916 (46 U.S.C.App. 822, 824, or 841a);

(ii) section 19 of the Merchant Marine Act, 1920 (46 U.S.C.App. 876);

(iii) section 2, 3, 4, or 5 of the Intercoastal Shipping Act, 1933 (46 U.S.C.App. 844, 845, 845a, or 845b);

(iv) section 14 or 17 of the Shipping Act of 1984 (46 U.S.C.App. 1713 or 1716); or

(v) section 2(d) or 3(d) of the Act of November 6, 1966 (46 U.S.C.App. 817d(d) or 817e(d);

(4) all final orders of the Atomic Energy Commission made reviewable by section 2239 of title 42;

(5) all rules, regulations, or final orders of the Interstate Commerce Commission made reviewable by section 2321 of this title and all final orders of such Commission made reviewable under section 11901(j)(2) of Title 49, United States Code; and

(6) all final orders under section 812 of the Fair Housing Act.

Jurisdiction is invoked by filing a petition as provided by section 2344 of this title.

APPENDIX 9:
DIRECTORY OF HUD FAIR HOUSING ENFORCEMENT CENTERS

REGION	ADDRESS	TELEPHONE	TTY
CONNECTICUT, MAINE, MASSACHU-SETTS, NEW HAMPSHIRE, RHODE IS-LAND, VERMONT	Fair Housing Enforcement Center, U.S. Department of Housing and Urban Development (HUD), 10 Causeway Street, Room 321, Boston, MA 02222-1092	617-565-5308/800-827-5005	617-565-5453
NEW JERSEY, NEW YORK	Fair Housing Enforcement Center, U.S. Department of Housing and Urban Development (HUD), 26 Federal Plaza, Room 3532, New York, NY 10278-0068	212-264-9610/800-496-4294	212-264-0927

DELAWARE, DISTRICT OF COLUMBIA, MARYLAND, PENNSYLVANIA, VIRGINIA, WEST VIRGINIA	Fair Housing Enforcement Center, U.S. Department of Housing and Urban Development (HUD), The Wanamaker Building, 100 Penn Square East, Philadelphia, PA 19107-3380	215-656-0660/888-799-2085	215-656-3450
ALABAMA, CARIBBEAN, FLORIDA, GEORGIA, KENTUCKY, MISSISSIPPI, NORTH CAROLINA, SOUTH CAROLINA, TENNESSEE	Fair Housing Enforcement Center, U.S. Department of Housing and Urban Development (HUD), Richard B. Russell Federal Building, 75 Spring Street SW, Room 230, Atlanta, GA 30303-3388	404-331-5140/800-440-8091	404-730-2654
ILLINOIS, INDIANA, MICHIGAN, MINNESOTA, OHIO, WISCONSIN	Fair Housing Enforcement Center, U.S. Department of Housing and Urban Development (HUD), Ralph H. Metcalfe Federal Building, 77 West Jackson Boulevard, Room 2101, Chicago, IL 60604-3507	312-353-7776/800-765-9372	312-353-7143
ARKANSAS, LOUISIANA, NEW MEXICO, OKLAHOMA, TEXAS	Fair Housing Enforcement Center, U.S. Department of Housing and Urban Development (HUD), 1600 Throckmorton, Room 502, Forth Worth, TX 76113-2905	817-978-9270/800-498-9371	817-978-9274

States	Address	Phone	Phone
IOWA, KANSAS, MISSOURI, NEBRASKA	Fair Housing Enforcement Center, U.S. Department of Housing and Urban Development (HUD), Gateway Tower II, 400 State Avenue, Room 200, Kansas City, KS 66101-2406	913-551-6958/800-743-5323	913-551-6972
COLORADO, MONTANA, NORTH DAKOTA, SOUTH DAKOTA, UTAH, WYOMING	Fair Housing Enforcement Center, U.S. Department of Housing and Urban Development (HUD), 633 17th Street, Denver, CO 80202-3607.	303-672-5437/800-877-7353	303-672-5248
ARIZONA, CALIFORNIA, HAWAII, NEVADA	Fair Housing Enforcement Center, U.S. Department of Housing and Urban Development (HUD), Phillip Burton Federal Building and U.S. Courthouse, 450 Golden Gate Avenue, San Francisco, CA 94102-3448	415-436-8400/800-347-3739	415-436-6594
ALASKA, IDAHO, OREGON, WASHINGTON	Fair Housing Enforcement Center, U.S. Department of Housing and Urban Development (HUD), Seattle Federal Office Building, 909 First Avenue, Room 205, Seattle, WA 98104-1000	206-220-5170/800-877-0246	206-220-5185

Source: United States Department of Housing and Urban Development

APPENDIX 10:
THE UNIFORM PLANNED COMMUNITY ACT

ARTICLE I: GENERAL PROVISIONS

§ 1-101. [Short Title] This Act shall be known and may be cited as the Uniform Planned Community Act.

§ 1-102. [Applicability]

(a) This Act applies to all planned communities created within this State after the effective date of this Act; but, if such a planned community:

(1) contains no more than 12 units, and is not subject to any development rights; or

(2) provides, in its declaration, that the annual average common expense liability of all units restricted to residential purposes, exclusive of optional user fees and any insurance premiums paid by the association, may not exceed $100, as adjusted pursuant to Section 1-115 [Adjustment of Dollar Amounts], it is subject only to Sections 1-105 [Separate Titles and Taxation], 1-106 [Applicability of Building Codes] and 1-107 [Eminent Domain] of this Act unless the declaration provides that the entire Act is applicable.

§ 1-103. [Definitions] In the declaration and bylaws, unless specifically provided otherwise or the context otherwise requires, and in this Act:

(1) "Affiliate of a declarant" means any person who controls, is controlled by, or is under common control with a declarant. A person "controls" a declarant if the person (i) is a general partner, officer, director, or employer of the declarant, (ii) directly or indirectly or acting in concert with one or more other persons, or through one or more subsidiaries, owns, controls, holds with power to vote, or holds proxies representing, more than 20 percent of the voting interest in the declarant, (iii) controls in any manner the election of a majority of the

---

directors of the declarant, or (iv) has contributed more than 20 percent of the capital of the declarant. A person "is controlled by" a declarant if the declarant (i) is a general partner, officer, director, or employer of the person, (ii) directly or indirectly or acting in concert with one or more other persons, or through one or more subsidiaries, owns, controls, holds with power to vote, or holds proxies representing, more than 20 percent of the voting interest in the person, (iii) controls in any manner the election of a majority of the directors of the person, or (iv) has contributed more than 20 percent of the capital of the person. Control does not exist if the powers described in this paragraph are held solely as security for an obligation and are not exercised.

(2) "Allocated interests" means the common expense liability and votes in the association allocated to each unit.

(3) "Association" or "unit owners association" means the unit owners association organized under Section 3-101.

(4) "Common elements" means any real estate within a planned community owned or leased by the association, other than a unit.

(5) "Common expenses" means expenditures made by or financial liabilities of the association, together with any allocations to reserves.

(6) "Common expense liability" means the liability for common expenses allocated to each unit pursuant to Section 2-107.

(7) "Condominium" means real estate, portions of which are designated for separate ownership and the remainder of which is designated for common ownership solely by the owners of those portions. Real estate is not a condominium unless the undivided interests in the common elements are vested in the unit owners.

(8) "Conversion building" means a building that at any time before creation of the planned community was occupied wholly or partially by persons other than purchasers and persons who occupy with the consent of purchasers.

(9) "Co-operative" means real estate owned by a corporation, trust, trustee, partnership, or unincorporated association, where the governing instruments of that organization provide that each of the organization's members, partners, stockholders or beneficiaries is entitled to exclusive occupancy of a designated portion of that real estate.

(10) "Declarant" means any person or group of persons acting in concert who (i) as part of a common promotional plan, offers to dispose of his or its interest in a unit not previously disposed of, [or] (ii) reserves or succeeds to any special declarant right [, or (iii) applies for registration of a planned community under Article 5.]

(11) "Declaration" means any instruments, however denominated, that create a planned community, and any amendments to those instruments.

(12) "Development rights" means any right or combination of rights reserved by a declarant in the declaration (i) to add real estate to a planned community; (ii) to create units, common elements, or limited common elements within a planned community; (iii) to subdivide units or convert units into common elements; or (iv) to withdraw real estate from a planned community.

(13) "Dispose" or "disposition" means a voluntary transfer to a purchaser of any legal or equitable interest in a unit, but does not include the transfer or release of a security interest.

(14) "Executive board" means the body, regardless of name, designated in the declaration to act on behalf of the association.

(15) "Identifying number" means a symbol or address that identifies only one unit in a planned community.

(16) "Leasehold planned community" means a planned community in which all or a portion of the real estate is subject to a lease the expiration or termination of which will terminate the planned community or reduce its size.

(17) "Limited common element" means a portion of the common elements allocated by the declaration or by operation of Section 2-102(2) or (4) for the exclusive use of one or more but fewer than all of the units.

(18) "Master association" means an organization described in Section 2-120, whether or not it is also an association described in Section 3-101.

(19) "Offering" means any advertisement, inducement, solicitation, or attempt to encourage any person to acquire any interest in a unit, other than as security for an obligation. An advertisement in a newspaper or other periodical of general circulation, or in any broadcast medium to the general public, of a planned community not located in this State, is not an offering if the advertisement states that an offering may be made only in compliance with the law of the jurisdiction in which the planned community is located.

(20) "Person" means a natural person, corporation, business trust, estate, trust, partnership, association, joint venture, government, governmental subdivision or agency, or other legal or commercial entity. [In the case of a land trust, however, "person" means the beneficiary of the trust rather than the trust or the trustee.]

(21) "Planned community" means real estate with respect to which any person, by virtue of his ownership of a unit, is obligated to pay for real property taxes, insurance, premiums, maintenance or improvement of other real estate described in a declaration. For purposes of this Act, neither a co-operative nor a condominium is a planned community, but real estate comprising a condominium or co-operative may be part of a planned community. "Ownership of a unit" does not include holding a leasehold interest of less than [20] years in a unit, including renewal options.

(22) "Purchaser" means any person, other than a declarant or a person in the business of selling real estate for his own account, who by means of a voluntary transfer acquires a legal or equitable interest in a unit, other than (i) a leasehold interest (including renewal options) of less than 20 years, or (ii) as security for an obligation.

(23) "Real estate" means any leasehold or other estate or interest in, over, or under land, including structures, fixtures, and other improvements and interests which by custom, usage, or law pass with a conveyance of land though not described in the contract of sale or instrument of conveyance. "Real estate" includes parcels with or without upper or lower boundaries, and spaces that may be filled with air or water.

(24) "Residential purposes" means use for dwelling or recreational purposes, or both.

(25) "Special declarant rights" means rights reserved for the benefit of a declarant (i) to complete improvements indicated on plats and plans filed with the declaration (Section 2-109); (ii) to exercise any development right (Section 2-110); (iii) to maintain sales offices, management offices, signs advertising the planned community, and models (Section 2-115); (iv) to use easements through the common elements for the purpose of making improvements within the planned community or within real estate which may be added to the planned community (Section 2-116); (v) to make the planned community part of a larger planned community or group of planned communities (Section 2-121); (vi) to make the planned community subject to a master association (Section 2-120); or (vii) to appoint or remove any officer or executive board member of the association or any master association during any period of declarant control (Section 3-103(c)).

(26) "Time share" means a right to occupy a unit or any of several units during [5] or more separated time periods over a period of at least [5] years, including renewal options, whether or not coupled with an estate or interest in a planned community or a specified portion thereof.

(27) "Unit" means a physical portion of the planned community designated for separate ownership or occupancy, the boundaries of which are described pursuant to Section 2-105(a)(5).

(28) "Unit owner" means a declarant or other person who owns a unit, or a lessee of a unit in a leasehold planned community whose lease expires simultaneously with any lease the expiration or termination of which will remove the unit from the planned community, but does not include a person having an interest in a unit solely as security for an obligation.

§ 1-108. [Supplemental General Principles of Law Applicable]

The principles of law and equity, including the law of corporations [and unincorporated associations], the law of real property and the law relative to capacity to contract, principal and agent, eminent domain, estoppel, fraud, misrepresentation, duress, coercion, mistake, receivership, substantial performance, or other validating or invalidating cause supplement the provisions of this Act, except to the extent inconsistent with this Act.

§ 1-112. [Unconscionable Agreement or Term of Contract]

(a) The court, upon finding as a matter of law that a contract or contract clause was unconscionable at the time the contract was made, may refuse to enforce the contract, enforce the remainder of the contract without the unconscionable clause, or limit the application of any unconscionable clause in order to avoid an unconscionable result.

(b) Whenever it is claimed, or appears to the court, that a contract or any contract clause is or may be unconscionable, the parties, in order to aid the court in making the determination, shall be afforded a reasonable opportunity to present evidence as to:

(1) the commercial setting of the negotiations;

(2) whether a party has knowingly taken advantage of the inability of the other party reasonably to protect his interests by reason of physical or mental infirmity, illiteracy, or inability to understand the language of the agreement or similar factors;

(3) the effect and purpose of the contract or clause; and

(4) if a sale, any gross disparity, at the time of contracting, between the amount charged for the real estate and the value of the real estate measured by the price at which similar real estate was readily obtainable in similar transactions, but a disparity between the contract price and the value of the real estate measured by the price at which similar real estate was readily obtainable in similar transactions does not, of itself, render the contract unconscionable.

§ 1-113. [Obligation of Good Faith] Every contract or duty governed by this Act imposes an obligation of good faith in its performance or enforcement.

ARTICLE 2: CREATION, ALTERATION, AND TERMINATION OF PLANNED COMMUNITIES

§ 2-101. [Creation of the Planned Community]

A planned community may be created pursuant to this Act only by recording a declaration executed in the same manner as a deed. The declaration must be recorded in every [county] in which any portion of the planned community is located, and must be indexed [in the Grantee's index] in the name of the planned community and the association and [in the Grantor's index] in the name of each person executing the declaration.

§ 2-102. [Unit Boundaries] Except as provided by the declaration:

(1) If walls, floors, or ceilings of a unit are designated as the boundaries of that unit, all lath, furring, wallboard, plasterboard, plaster, paneling, tiles, wallpaper, paint, finished flooring, and any other materials constituting any part of the finished surfaces thereof are a part of the unit, and all other portions of the walls, floors, or ceilings are a part of the common elements.

(2) If any chute, flue, duct, wire, conduit, bearing wall, bearing column, or any other fixture lies partially within and partially outside the designated boundaries of a unit, any portion thereof serving only that unit is a limited common element allocated solely to that unit, and any portion thereof serving more than one unit or any portion of the common elements is a part of the common elements.

(3) Subject to the provisions of paragraph (2), all spaces, interior partitions, and other fixtures and improvements within the boundaries of a unit are a part of the unit.

(4) Any shutters, awnings, window boxes, doorsteps, stoops, porches, balconies, patios, and all exterior doors and windows or other fixtures designed to serve a single unit, but located outside the unit's boundaries, are limited common elements allocated exclusively to that unit.

§ 2-103. [Construction and Validity of Declaration and Bylaws]

(a) All provisions of the declaration and bylaws are severable.

(b) The rule against perpetuities may not be applied to defeat any provision of the declaration, bylaws, rules, or regulations adopted pursuant to Section 3-102(a)(1).

(c) In the event of a conflict between the provisions of the declaration and the bylaws, the declaration prevails except to the extent the declaration is inconsistent with this Act.

(d) Title to a unit and common elements is not rendered unmarketable or otherwise affected by reason of an insubstantial failure of the declaration to comply with this Act. Whether a substantial failure impairs marketability of title is not affected by this Act.

§ 2-104. [Description of Units]

A description of a unit which sets forth the name of the planned community, the [recording data] for the declaration, the [county] in which the planned community is located, and the identifying number of the unit, is a sufficient legal description of that unit and all rights, obligations, and interests appurtenant to that unit which were created by the declaration or bylaws.

§ 2-105. [Contents of Declaration]

(a) The declaration for a planned community must contain:

(1) the names of the planned community and the association;

(2) the name of every [county] in which any part of the planned community is situated;

(3) a legally sufficient description of the real estate included in the planned community;

(4) a statement of the maximum number of units which the declarant reserves the right to create;

(5) a description of the boundaries of each unit created by the declaration, including the unit's identifying number;

(6) a description of any real estate which is or must become common elements and limited common elements, other than those specified in Section 2-102(2) and (4), as provided in Section 2-109(b)(10);

(7) a description of any real estate (except real estate subject to development rights) which may be allocated subsequently as limited common elements, other than limited common elements specified in Section 2-102(2) and (4), together with a statement that they may be so allocated;

(8) a description of any development rights and other special declarant rights (Section 1-103(25)) reserved by the declarant, together with a legally sufficient description of the real estate to which each of those rights applies, and a time limit within which each of those rights must be exercised;

(9) if any development right may be exercised with respect to different parcels of the real estate at different times, a statement to that effect together with (i) either a statement fixing the boundaries of those portions and regulating the order in which those portions may be subjected to the exercise of each development right, or a statement that no assurances are made in those regards, and (ii) a statement as to whether, if any development right is exercised in any portion of the real estate subject to that development right, that development right must be exercised in all or in any other portion of the remainder of that real estate;

(10) any other conditions or limitations under which the rights described in paragraph (8) may be exercised or will lapse;

(11) an allocation to each unit of the allocated interests in the manner described in Section 2-107;

(12) any restrictions on use, occupancy, and alienation of the units;

(13) the [recording data] for recorded easements and licenses appurtenant to or included in the planned community or to which any portion of the planned community is or may become subject by virtue of a reservation in the declaration; and

(14) all matters required by Sections 2-106, 2-107, 2-108, 2-109, 2-115, 2-116, and 3-103(d).

(b) The declaration may contain any other matters the declarant deems appropriate.

§ 2-107. [Allocation of Votes and Common Expense Liabilities]

(a) The declaration shall allocate a fraction or percentage of the common expenses of the association (Section 3-115(a)), and a portion of the votes in the association to each unit in the planned community, and state the formulas used to establish those allocations. Those allocations may not discriminate in favor of units owned by the declarant.

(b) If units may be added to or withdrawn from the planned community, the declaration must state the formulas to be used to reallocate the allocated interests among all units included in the planned community after the addition or withdrawal.

(c) The declaration may provide: (i) that different allocations of votes shall be made to the units on particular matters specified in the declaration; (ii) for cumulative voting only for the purpose of electing members of the executive board; and (iii) for class voting on specified issues affecting the class if necessary to protect valid interests of the class. A declarant may not utilize cumulative or class voting for the purpose of evading any limitation imposed on declarants by this Act, nor may units constitute a class because they are owned by a declarant.

(d) Except for minor variations due to rounding, the sum of the common expense liabilities allocated at any time to all the units must equal one if stated as a fraction or 100 percent if stated as a percentage. In the event of a discrepancy between an allocated interest and the result derived from application of the pertinent formula, the allocated interest prevails.

§ 2-111. [Alterations of Units] Subject to the provisions of the declaration and other provisions of law, a unit owner:

(1) may make any improvements or alterations to his unit that do not impair the structural integrity or mechanical systems or lessen the support of any portion of the planned community;

(2) may not change the appearance of the common elements, or the exterior appearance of a unit or any other portion of the planned community, without permission of the association;

(3) after acquiring an adjoining unit or an adjoining part of an adjoining unit, may remove or alter any intervening partition or create apertures therein, even if the partition in whole or in part is a common element, if those acts do not impair the structural integrity or mechanical systems or lessen the support of any portion of the planned community. Removal of partitions or creation of apertures under this paragraph is not an alteration of boundaries.

§ 2-116. [Easement Rights]

(a) Subject to the provisions of Section 3-112, (Alienation of Common Elements) the unit owners have an easement (i) in the common elements for purposes of access to their units and (ii) to use the common elements and all real estate which must become common elements (Section 2-105(a)(7)) for all other purposes.

(b) Subject to the provisions of the declaration, a declarant has an easement through the common elements as may be reasonably necessary for the purpose of discharging a declarant's obligations or exercising special declarant rights, whether arising under this Act or reserved in the declaration.

§ 2-118. [Termination of Planned Community]

(a) Except in the case of a taking of all the units by eminent domain (Section 1-107), a planned community may be terminated only by agreement of unit owners of units to which at least 80 percent of the votes in the association are allocated, or any larger percentage the declaration specifies. The declaration may specify a smaller percentage only if all of the units in the planned community are restricted exclusively to non-residential uses.

(b) An agreement to terminate must be evidenced by the execution of a termination agreement, or ratifications thereof, in the same manner as a deed, by the requisite number of unit owners. The termination agreement must specify a date after which the agreement will be void unless it is recorded before that date. A termination agreement and all ratifications thereof must be recorded in every [county] in which a portion of the planned community is situated, and is effective only upon recordation.

(c) In the case of a planned community containing only units having horizontal boundaries described in the declaration, a termination agreement may provide that all the common elements and units of the planned community shall be sold following termination. If, pursuant to the agreement, any real estate in the planned community is to be sold following termination, the termination agreement must set forth the minimum terms of the sale.

(d) In the case of a planned community containing any units not having horizontal boundaries described in the declaration, a termination agreement may provide for sale of the common elements, but may not require that the units be sold following termination, unless the declaration as originally recorded provided otherwise or unless all the unit owners consent to the sale.

(e) The association, on behalf of the unit owners, may contract for the sale of real estate in the planned community, but the contract is not binding until approved pursuant to subsections (a) and (b). If any real estate in the planned community is to be sold following termination, title to that real estate, upon termination, vests in the association as trustee for the holders of all interests in the units. Thereafter, the association has all powers necessary and appropriate of effect the sale. Until the sale has been concluded and the proceeds thereof distributed, the association continues in existence with all powers it had before termination. Proceeds of the sale must be distributed to unit owners and lien holders as their interests may appear, in proportion to the respective interests of unit owners as provided in subsection (h). Unless otherwise specified in the termination agreement, as long as the association holds title to the real estate, each unit owner and his successors in interest have an exclusive right to occupancy of the portion of the real estate that formerly constituted his unit. During the period of that occupancy, each unit owner and his successors in interest remain liable for all assessments and other obligations imposed on unit owners by this Act or the declaration.

(f) If the real estate constituting the planned community is not to be sold following termination, title to the common elements and, in a planned community containing only units having horizontal boundaries described in the declaration, title to all the real estate in the planned community, vests in the unit owners upon termination as tenants in common in proportion to their respective interests as provided in subsection (h), and liens on the units shift accordingly. While the tenancy in common exists, each unit owner and his successors in interest have an exclusive right to occupancy of the portion of the real estate that formerly constituted his unit.

(g) Following termination of the planned community, the proceeds of any sale of real estate, together with the assets of the association, are held by the association as trustee for unit owners and holders of liens on the units as their interests may appear. Following termination, creditors of the association holding liens on the units which were [recorded] [docketed] [(insert other procedures required under state law to perfect a lien on real estate as a result of a judgment)] before termination may enforce those liens in the same manner as any lien holder. All other creditors of the association are to be treated as if they had perfected liens on the units immediately before termination.

(h) The respective interests of unit owners referred to in subsections (e), (f) and (g) are as follows:

(1) Except as provided in paragraph (2), the respective interests of unit owners are the fair market values of their units and limited common elements immediately before the termination, as determined by one or more independent appraisers selected by the association. The decision of the independent appraisers shall be distributed to the unit owners and becomes final unless disapproved within 30 days after distribution by unit owners of units to which 25 percent of the votes in the association are allocated. The proportion of any unit owner's interest to that of all unit owners is determined by dividing the fair market value of that unit owner's unit by the total fair market values of all the units and common elements.

(2) If any unit or any limited common element is destroyed to the extent that an appraisal of the fair market value thereof before destruction cannot be made, the interests of all unit owners are their respective common expense liabilities immediately before the termination.

(i) Except as provided in subsection (j), foreclosure or enforcement of a lien or encumbrance against the entire planned community does not of itself terminate the planned community, and foreclosure or enforcement of a lien or encumbrance against a portion of the planned community does not of itself withdraw that portion from the planned community. Foreclosure or enforcement of a lien or encumbrance against withdrawable real estate does not of itself withdraw that real estate from the planned community, but the person taking title thereto has the right to require from the association, upon request, an amendment excluding the real estate from the planned community.

(j) If a lien or encumbrance against a portion of the real estate comprising the planned community has priority over the declaration, and the lien or encumbrance has not been partially released, the parties foreclosing the lien or encumbrance may upon foreclosure, record an instrument excluding the real estate subject to that lien or encumbrance from the planned community.

ARTICLE 3: MANAGEMENT OF PLANNED COMMUNITY

§ 3-101. [Organization of Unit Owners' Association]

A unit owners' association must be organized no later than the date the first unit in the planned community is conveyed. The membership of the association at all times shall consist exclusively of all the unit owners or, following termination of the planned community, of all unit owners entitled to distributions of proceeds under Section 2-118 or their heirs, successors, or assigns. The association shall be organized as a profit or nonprofit corporation [or as an unincorporated association.]

§ 3-102. [Powers of Unit Owners' Association]

(a) Except as provided in subsection (b), and subject to the provisions of the declaration, the association [, even if unincorporated,] may:

(1) adopt and amend bylaws and rules and regulations;

(2) adopt and amend budgets for revenues, expenditures, and reserves and collect assessments for common expenses from unit owners;

(3) hire and discharge managing agents and other employees, agents, and independent contractors;

(4) institute, defend, or intervene in litigation or administrative proceedings in its own name on behalf of itself or 2 or more unit owners on matters affecting the planned community;

(5) make contracts and incur liabilities;

(6) regulate the use, maintenance, repair, replacement, and modification of common elements;

(7) cause additional improvements to be made as a part of the common elements;

(8) acquire, hold, encumber, and convey in its own name any right, title, or interest to real or personal property, but common elements may be conveyed or subjected to a security interest only pursuant to Section 3-112;

(9) grant easements, leases, licenses, and concessions through or over the common elements;

(10) impose and receive any payments, fees, or charges for the use, rental, or operation of the common elements (other than the limited common elements described in Sections 2-102(2) and (4)) and for services provided to unit owners;

(11) impose charges for late payment of assessments and, after notice and an opportunity to be heard, levy reasonable fines for violations of the declaration, bylaws, and rules and regulations of the association;

(12) impose reasonable charges for the preparation and recordation of amendments to the declaration, resale certificates required by Section 4-109, or statements of unpaid assessments;

(13) provide for the indemnification of its officers and executive board and maintain directors' and officers' liability insurance;

(14) assign its right to future income, including the right to receive common expense assessments, but only to the extent the declaration expressly so provides;

(15) exercise any other powers conferred by the declaration or bylaws;

(16) exercise all other powers that may be exercised in this State by legal entities of the same type as the association; and

(17) exercise any other powers necessary and proper for the governance and operation of the association.

(b) The declaration may not impose limitations on the power of the association to deal with a declarant which are more restrictive than the limitations imposed on the power of the association to deal with other persons.

§ 3-103. [Executive Board Members and Officers]

(a) Except as provided in the declaration, the bylaws, in subsection (b), or other provisions of this Act, the executive board may act in all instances on behalf of the association. In the performance of their duties, officers and members of the executive board are required to exercise

(i) if appointed by the declarant, the care required of fiduciaries of the unit owners and (ii) if elected by the unit owners, ordinary and reasonable care.

(b) The executive board may not act on behalf of the association to amend the declaration (Section 2-117), to terminate the planned community (Section 2-118), or to elect members of the executive board or determine the qualifications, powers and duties, or terms of office of executive board members (Section 3-103(f)), but the executive board may fill vacancies in its membership for the unexpired portion of any term.

(c) Within [30] days after adoption of any proposed budget for the planned community, the executive board shall provide a summary of the budget to all the unit owners, and shall set a date for a meeting of the unit owners to consider ratification of the budget not less than 14 nor more than 30 days after mailing of the summary. Unless at that meeting a majority of all the unit owners or any larger vote specified in the declaration reject the budget, the budget is ratified, whether or not a quorum is present. In the event the proposed budget is rejected, the periodic budget last ratified by the unit owners shall be continued until such time as the unit owners ratify a subsequent budget proposed by the executive board.

(d) Subject to subsection (e), the declaration may provide for a period of declarant control of the association, during which period a declarant, or persons designated by him, may appoint and remove the officers and members of the executive board. Regardless of the period provided in the declaration, a period of declarant control terminates no later than the earlier of: (i) [60] days after conveyance of [75] percent of the units which may be created to unit owners other than a declarant; (ii) [2] years after all declarants have ceased to offer units for sale in the ordinary course of business; or (iii) [2] years after any development right to add new units was last exercised. A declarant may voluntarily surrender the right to appoint and remove officers and members of the executive board before termination of that period, but in that event he may require, for the duration of the period of declarant control, that specified actions of the association or executive board, as described in a recorded instrument executed by the declarant, be approved by the declarant before they become effective.

(e) Not later than [60] days after conveyance of [25] percent of the units which may be created to unit owners other than a declarant, at least one member and not less than [25] percent of the members of the executive board must be elected by unit owners other than the declarant. Not later than [60] days after conveyance of [50] percent of the units which may be created to unit owners other than a declarant, not less than [331/3] percent of the members of the executive board must be elected by unit owners other than the declarant.

(f) Not later than the termination of any period of declarant control, the unit owners shall elect an executive board of at least 3 members, at least a majority of whom must be unit owners. The executive board shall elect the officers. The executive board members and officers shall take office upon election.

(g) Notwithstanding any provision of the declaration or bylaws to the contrary, the unit owners, by a two-thirds vote of all persons present and entitled to vote at any meeting of the unit owners at which a quorum is present, may remove any member of the executive board with or without cause, other than a member appointed by the declarant.

§ 3-106. [Bylaws]

(a) The bylaws of the association must provide for:

(1) the number of members of the executive board and the titles of the officers of the association;

(2) election by the executive board of a president, treasurer, secretary, and any other officers of the association the bylaws specify;

(3) the qualifications, powers and duties, terms of office, and manner of electing and removing executive board members and officers and filling vacancies;

(4) which, if any, of its powers the executive board or officers may delegate to other persons or to a managing agent;

(5) which of its officers may prepare, execute, certify, and record amendments to the declaration on behalf of the association; and

(6) the method of amending the bylaws.

(b) Subject to the provisions of the declaration, the bylaws may provide for any other matters the association deems necessary and appropriate.

§ 3-107. [Upkeep of Planned Community]

(a) Except to the extent provided by the declaration, subsection (b), or Section 3-113(h), the association is responsible for maintenance, repair, and replacement of the common elements, and each unit owner is responsible for maintenance, repair, and replacement of his unit. Each unit owner shall afford to the association and the other unit owners, and to their agents or employees, access through his unit reasonably necessary for those purposes. If damage is inflicted on the common elements, or on any unit through which access is taken, the unit owner responsible for the damage, or the association if it is responsible, is liable for the prompt repair thereof.

(b) In addition to the liability that a declarant as a unit owner has under this Act, the declarant alone is liable for all expenses in connection with real estate subject to development rights. No other unit owner and no other portion of the planned community is subject to a claim for payment of those expenses. Unless the declaration provides otherwise, any income or proceeds from real estate subject to development rights inures to the declarant. In the event all development rights have expired with respect to any real estate, the declarant remains liable for all expenses of that real estate unless, upon expiration, the declaration provides that such real estate becomes common elements or units.

§ 3-113. [Insurance]

(a) Commencing not later than the time of the first conveyance of a unit to a person other than a declarant, the association shall maintain, to the extent reasonably available:

(1) property insurance on the common elements and on property which must become common elements insuring against all risks of direct physical loss commonly insured against or, in the case of a conversion building, against fire and extended coverage perils. The total amount of insurance after application of any deductibles shall be not less than 80 percent of the actual cash value of the insured property at the time the insurance is purchased and at each renewal date, exclusive of land, excavations, foundations, and other items normally excluded from property policies; and

(2) liability insurance, including medical payments insurance, in an amount determined by the executive board but not less than any amount specified in the declaration, covering all occurrences commonly insured against for death, bodily injury, and property damage arising out of or in connection with the use, ownership, or maintenance of the common elements.

(b) In the case of a building containing units having horizontal boundaries described in the declaration, the insurance maintained under subsection (a) (1), to the extent reasonably available, shall include the units, but need not include improvements and betterments installed by unit owners.

(c) If the insurance described in subsections (a) and (b) is not reasonably available, the association promptly shall cause notice of that fact to be hand-delivered or sent prepaid by United States mail to all unit owners. The declaration may require the association to carry any other insurance, and the association in any event may carry any other insurance it deems appropriate to protect the association or the unit owners.

(d) Insurance policies carried pursuant to subsections (a) and (b) must provide that:

(1) each unit owner is an insured person under the policy with respect to liability arising out of his interest in the common elements or membership in the association;

(2) the insurer waives its right to subrogation under the policy against any unit owner or member of his household;

(3) no act or omission by any unit owner, unless acting within the scope of his authority on behalf of the association, will void the policy or be a condition to recovery under the policy; and

(4) if, at the time of a loss under the policy, there is other insurance in the name of a unit owner covering the same risk covered by the policy, the association's policy provides primary insurance.

(e) Any loss covered by the property policy under subsections (a)(1) and (b) must be adjusted with the association, but the insurance proceeds for that loss are payable to any insurance trustee designated for that purpose, or otherwise to the association, and not to any mortgagee or beneficiary under a deed of trust. The insurance trustee or the association shall hold any insurance proceeds in trust for unit owners and lien holders as their interests may appear. Subject to the provisions of subsection (h), the proceeds must be disbursed first for the repair or restoration of the damaged property, and unit owners and lien holders are not entitled to receive payment of any portion of the proceeds unless there is a surplus of proceeds after the property has been completely repaired or restored, or the planned community is terminated.

(f) An insurance policy issued to the association does not prevent a unit owner from obtaining insurance for his own benefit.

(g) An insurer that has issued an insurance policy under this section shall issue certificates or memoranda of insurance to the association and, upon written request, to any unit owner, mortgagee, or beneficiary under a deed of trust. The insurer issuing the policy may not cancel or refuse to renew it until [30] days after notice of the proposed cancellation or non-renewal has been mailed to the association, each unit owner and each mortgagee or beneficiary under a deed of trust to whom a certificate or memorandum of insurance have been issued at their respective last known addresses.

(h) Any portion of the planned community for which insurance is required under this section which is damaged or destroyed shall be repaired or replaced promptly by the association unless (i) the planned community is terminated, (ii) repair or replacement would be illegal under any state or local health or safety statute or ordinance, or (iii) [80] percent of the unit owners, including every owner of a unit or assigned limited common element which will not be rebuilt, vote not to rebuild. The cost of repair or replacement in excess of insurance proceeds and reserves is a common expense. If the entire planned community is not repaired or replaced, (i) the insurance proceeds attributable to the damaged common elements must be used to restore the damaged area to a condition compatible with the remainder of the planned community, (ii) the insurance proceeds attributable to units and limited common elements which are not rebuilt must be distributed to the owners of those units and the owners of the units to which those limited common elements were allocated, or to lienholders, as their interests may appear, and (iii) the remainder of the proceeds must be distributed to all the unit owners or lienholders, as their interests may appear, in proportion to the common expense liabilities of all the units. If the unit owners vote not to rebuild any unit, that unit's allocated interests are automatically reallocated upon the vote as if the unit had been condemned under Section 1-107(a), and the association promptly shall prepare, execute, and record an amendment to the declaration reflecting the reallocations. Notwithstanding the provisions of this subsection, Section 2-118 (termination of the planned community) governs the distribution of insurance proceeds if the planned community is terminated.

(i) The provisions of this section may be varied or waived in the case of a planned community all of whose units are restricted to non-residential use.

§ 3-115. [Assessments for Common Expenses]

(a) Until the association makes a common expense assessment, the declarant shall pay all common expenses. After any assessment has been made by the association, assessments must be made at least annually, based on a budget adopted at least annually by the association.

(b) Except for assessments under subsections (c), (d), and (e), all common expenses must be assessed against all the units in accordance with the allocation set forth in the declaration pursuant to Section 2-107(a). Any past due common expense assessment or instalment thereof bears interest at the rate established by the association not exceeding [18] percent per year.

(c) To the extent required by the declaration:

(1) any common expense associated with the maintenance, repair, or replacement of a limited common element must be assessed against the units to which that limited common element is assigned, equally, or in any other proportion that the declaration provides;

(2) any common expense or portion thereof benefiting fewer than all of the units must be assessed exclusively against the units benefited; and

(3) the costs of insurance must be assessed in proportion to risk and the costs of utilities must be assessed in proportion to usage.

(d) Assessments to pay a judgment against the association (Section 3-117 (a)) may be made only against the units in the planned community at the time the judgment was entered, in proportion to their common expense liabilities.

(e) If any common expense is caused by the misconduct of any unit owner, the association may assess that expense exclusively against his unit.

(f) If common expense liabilities are reallocated, common expense assessments and any instalment thereof not yet due shall be recalculated in accordance with the reallocated common expense liabilities.

§ 3-116. [Lien for Assessments]

(a) The association has a lien on a unit for any assessment levied against that unit for fines imposed against its unit owner from the time the assessment or fine becomes due. The association's lien may be foreclosed in like manner as a mortgage on real estate [or a power of sale under (insert appropriate state statute)] [but the association shall give reasonable notice of its action to all lienholders of the unit whose interest would be affected]. Unless the declaration otherwise provides, fees, charges, late charges, fines, and interest charged pursuant to Section 3-102(a)(10), (11) and (12) are enforceable as assessments under this section. If an assessment is payable in instalments, the full amount of the assessment is a lien from the time the first instalment thereof becomes due.

(b) A lien under this section is prior to all other liens and encumbrances on a unit except (i) liens and encumbrances recorded before the recordation of the declaration, (ii) a first mortgage or deed of trust on the unit recorded before the date on which the assessment sought to be enforced became delinquent, and (iii) liens for real estate taxes and other governmental assessments or charges against the unit. The lien is also prior to the mortgages and deeds of trust described in clause (ii) above to the extent of the common expense assessments based on the periodic budget adopted by the association pursuant to Section 3-115(a) which would have become due in the absence of acceleration during the 6 months immediately preceding institution of an action to enforce the lien. This subsection does not affect the priority of mechanics' or materialmen's liens, or the priority of liens for other assessments made by the association. [The lien under this section is not subject to the provisions of (insert appropriate reference to state homestead, dower and curtesy, or other exemptions).]

(c) Unless the declaration otherwise provides, if 2 or more associations have liens for assessments created at any time on the same real estate, those liens have equal priority.

(d) Recording of the declaration constitutes record notice and perfection of the lien. No further recordation of any claim of lien for assessment under this section is required.

(e) A lien for unpaid assessments is extinguished unless proceedings to enforce the lien are instituted within [3] years after the full amount of the assessments becomes due.

(f) This section does not prohibit actions to recover sums for which subsection (a) creates a lien, or prohibit an association from taking a deed in lieu of foreclosure.

(g) A judgment or decree in any action brought under this section must include costs and reasonable attorney's fees for the prevailing party.

(h) The association upon written request shall furnish to a unit owner a recordable statement setting forth the amount of unpaid assessments against his unit. The statement must be furnished within [10] business days after receipt of the request and is binding on the association, the executive board, and every unit owner.

ARTICLE 4: PROTECTION OF PURCHASERS

§ 4-103. [Public Offering Statement: General Provisions]

(a) Except as provided in subsection (b), a public offering statement must contain a fully and accurately disclose:

(1) the names and principal addresses of the declarant and of the planned community;

(2) a general description of the planned community, including, to the extent possible, the types, number, and declarant's schedule of commencement and completion of construction of buildings and amenities that declarant anticipates including in the planned community;

(3) the number of units in the planned community;

(4) copies and a brief narrative description of the significant features of the declaration (other than the plats and plans) and any other recorded covenants, conditions, restrictions and reservations affecting the planned community; the bylaws, and any rules or regulations of the association; copies of any contracts and leases to be signed by purchasers at closing; and a brief narrative description of any contracts or leases that will or may be subject to cancellation by the association under Section 3-105;

(5) any current balance sheet and a projected budget for the association, either within or as an exhibit to the public offering statement, for [one] year after the date of the first conveyance to a purchaser, and thereafter the current budget of the association, a statement of who prepared the budget, and a statement of the budget's assumptions concerning occupancy and inflation factors. The budget must include, without limitation:

(i) a statement of the amount, or a statement that there is no amount, included in the budget as a reserve for repairs and replacement;

(ii) a statement of any other reserves;

(iii) the projected common expense assessment by category of expenditures for the association; and

(iv) the projected monthly common expenses assessment for each type of unit;

(6) any services not reflected in the budget that the declarant provides, or expenses that he pays, and that he expects may become at any subsequent time a common expense of the association and the projected common expense assessment attributable to each of those services or expenses for the association and for each type of unit;

(7) any initial or special fee due from the purchaser at closing, together with a description of the purpose and method of calculating the fee;

(8) a description of any liens, defects, or encumbrances on or affecting the title to the planned community;

(9) a description of any financing offered or arranged by the declarant;

(10) the terms and significant limitations of any warranties provided by the declarant, including statutory warranties and limitations on the enforcement thereof or on damages;

(11) a statement that:

(i) within 15 days after receipt of a public offering statement a purchaser, before conveyance, may cancel any contract for purchase of a unit from a declarant,

(ii) if a declarant fails to provide a public offering statement to a purchaser before conveying a unit, that purchaser may recover from the declarant [10] percent of the sales price of the unit, and

(iii) if a purchaser receives the public offering statement more than 15 days before signing a contract, he cannot cancel the contract;

(12) a statement of any unsatisfied judgments or pending suits against the association, and the status of any pending suits material to the planned community of which a declarant has actual knowledge;

(13) a statement that any deposit made in connection with the purchase of a unit will be held in an escrow until closing and will be returned to the purchaser if the purchaser cancels the contract pursuant to Section 4-108, together with the name and address of the escrow agent;

(14) any restraints on alienation of any portion of the planned community;

(15) a description of the insurance coverage provided for the benefit of unit owners;

(16) any current or expected fees or charges to be paid by unit owners for the use of any common elements and other facilities related to the planned community;

(17) the extent to which financial arrangements have been provided for completion of all improvements labeled "MUST BE BUILT" pursuant to Section 4-119 (Declarant's Obligation to Complete and Restore);

(18) a brief narrative description of any zoning and other land use requirements affecting the planned community; and

(19) all unusual and material circumstances, features, and characteristics of the planned community and the units.

(b) If a planned community composed of not more than 12 units is not subject to any development rights, and no power is reserved to a declarant to make the planned community part of a larger planned community, group of planned communities, or other real estate, a public offering statement may but need not include the information otherwise required by paragraphs (9), (10), (15), (16), (17), (18) and (19) of subsection (a), and the narrative descriptions of documents required by paragraph (a)(4).

(c) A declarant promptly shall amend the public offering statement to report any material change in the information required by this section.

§ 4-108. [Purchaser's Right to Cancel]

(a) A person required to deliver a public offering statement pursuant to Section 4-102(c) shall provide a purchaser with the public offering statement and all amendments thereto before conveyance of that unit, and not later than the date of any contract of sale. Unless a purchaser is given the public offering statement more than 15 days before execution of a contract for the purchase of a unit, the purchaser, before conveyance, may cancel the contract within 15 days after first receiving the public offering statement.

(b) If a purchaser elects to cancel a contract pursuant to subsection (a), he may do so by hand-delivering notice thereof to the offeror or by mailing notice thereof by prepaid United States mail to the offeror or to his agent for service of process. Cancellation is without penalty, and all payments made by the purchaser before cancellation shall be refunded promptly.

(c) If a person required to deliver a public offering statement pursuant to Section 4-102(c) fails to provide a purchaser to whom a unit is conveyed with that public offering statement and all amendments thereto as required by subsection (a), the purchaser, in addition to any rights to damages or other relief, is entitled to receive from that person an amount equal to [10] percent of the sales price of the unit.

§ 4-109. [Resales of Units]

(a) Except in the case of a sale where delivery of a public offering statement is required, or unless exempt under Section 4-101(b), a unit owner shall furnish to a purchaser before execution of any contract for sale of a unit, or otherwise before conveyance, a copy of the declaration (other than the plats and plans), the bylaws, the rules or regulations of the association, and a certificate containing:

(1) a statement disclosing the effect on the proposed disposition of any right of first refusal or other restraint on the free alienability of the unit;

(2) a statement setting forth the amount of the monthly common expense assessment and any unpaid common expense or special assessment currently due and payable from the selling unit owner;

(3) a statement of any other fees payable by unit owners;

(4) a statement of any capital expenditures anticipated by the association for the current and 2 next succeeding fiscal years;

(5) a statement of the amount of any reserves for capital expenditures and of any portions of those reserves designated by the association for any specified projects;

(6) the most recent regularly prepared balance sheet and income and expense statement, if any, of the association;

(7) the current operating budget of the association;

(8) a statement of any unsatisfied judgments against the association and the status of any pending suits in which the association is a defendant;

(9) a statement describing any insurance coverage provided for the benefit of unit owners;

(10) a statement as to whether the executive board has knowledge that any alterations or improvements to the unit or to any limited common elements assigned thereto violate any provision of the declaration;

(11) a statement as to whether the executive board has knowledge of any violations of the health or building codes with respect to the unit, the limited common elements assigned thereto, or any other portion of the planned community; and

(12) a statement of the remaining term of any leasehold estate affecting the planned community and the provisions governing any extension or renewal thereof.

(b) The association, within 10 days after a request by a unit owner shall furnish a certificate containing the information necessary to enable the unit owner to comply with this section. A unit owner providing a certificate pursuant to subsection (a) is not liable to the purchaser for any erroneous information provided by the association and included in the certificate.

(c) A purchaser is not liable for any unpaid assessment or fee greater than the amount set forth in the certificate prepared by the association. A unit owner is not liable to a purchaser for the failure or delay of the association to provide the certificate in a timely manner, but the purchase contract is voidable by the purchaser until the certificate has been provided and for [5] days thereafter or until conveyance, whichever first occurs.

§ 4-117. [Effect of Violations on Rights of Action; Attorney's Fees]

If a declarant or any other person subject to this Act fails to comply with any provision hereof or any provision of the declaration or by-laws, any person or class of persons adversely affected by the failure to comply has a claim for appropriate relief. Punitive damages may be awarded for a willful failure to comply with this Act. The court, in an appropriate case, may award reasonable attorney's fees.

GLOSSARY

Acceptance For Filing—The formal act by which the governing official authorizes the public offering of interests in a plan for a cooperative, condominium or homeowners' association.

Acceptance of Deed—The physical taking of the deed by the grantee.

Acceptance of Offer—The seller's agreement to the terms of the agreement of sale.

Accrued Interest—Interest earned but not yet paid.

Agreement of Sale—Contract signed by buyer and seller stating the terms and conditions under which a property will be sold.

Alteration Agreement—Agreement that describes the terms under which the cooperative gives permission to a shareholder before making any changes or improvements to the unit the member occupies, also referred to as an improvement agreement.

Alternative Documentation—A method of documenting a loan file that relies on information the borrower is likely to be able to provide instead of waiting on verification sent to third parties for confirmation of statements made in the application.

Amortization—Repayment of a loan with periodic payments of both principal and interest calculated to payoff the loan at the end of a fixed period of time.

Annual Membership Meeting—Yearly meeting to which all the members of the co-op are invited during which members elect the board of directors, bylaw revisions are voted on, and other important matters are discussed.

Annual Percentage Rate (APR)—The cost of credit expressed as a yearly rate. The annual percentage rate is often not the same as the interest rate. It is a percentage that results from an equation considering the amount financed, the finance charges, and the term of the loan.

Articles of Incorporation—The legal document that establishes the existence and purpose of the cooperative corporation.

Assignment—The transfer of ownership, rights, or interests in property by one person, the assignor, to another, the assignee.

Balloon Mortgage—Balloon mortgage loans are short-term fixed-rate loans with fixed monthly payments for a set number of years followed by one large final "balloon" payment for all of the remainder of the principal.

Black Book—The offering plan used by the sponsor as the sales document for a cooperative, condominium or homeowner's association.

Blanket Mortgage—A single loan covering an entire building or the entire property that the cooperative owns.

BMIR—An FHA abbreviation for Below Market Interest Rate. This term applies to certain FHA mortgage insurance programs where the mortgage carries with it a subsidized interest rate that is below the market. This reduces monthly cost and makes it possible for low to moderate income families to benefit from the cooperative form of home ownership.

Board of Directors—Individuals elected by the co-op's members/shareholders to govern the cooperative, including setting policy, making rules and regulations and other decisions which govern the operations and the welfare of its members/shareholders.

Borrower—Also known as the mortgagor, refers to the individual who applies for and receives funds in the form of a loan and is obligated to repay the loan in full under the terms of the loan.

Bylaws—A written set of provisions and directions that the cooperative corporation follows in governing operations.

Capacity—Your ability to make your mortgage payments on time. This depends on your income and income stability, your assets and reserves, and the amount of your income each month that is available after you have paid for your housing costs, debts and other obligations.

Carrying Charges—Payments a condominium owner must make, including his mortgage and real estate taxes, also referred to as monthly carrying charges.

Certificate of Title—Written opinion of the status of title to a property, given by an attorney or title company. This certificate does not offer the protection given by title insurance.

Chain of Title—The chronological order of conveyance of a property from the original owner to the present owner.

Closing—Also known as settlement, refers to the conclusion of a real estate transaction and includes the delivery of the security instrument, signing of legal documents and the disbursement of the funds necessary to the sale of the home or loan transaction.

Closing Agent—A person that coordinates closing-related activities, such as recording the closing documents and disbursing funds.

Closing Costs—Also known as settlement costs, refers to the costs for services that must be performed before the loan can be initiated, such as title fees, recording fees, appraisal fee, credit report fee, pest inspection, attorney's fees, and surveying fees.

Closing Date—In a condominium, the date on which title to property passes from the seller to the buyer. In the case of most cooperatives, the date on which title passes from the sponsor to the cooperative corporation, and the approximate date the shares are issued to the individual purchasers.

Collateral—Assets pledged as security for a debt, such as a home.

Commitment—A promise to lend and a statement by the lender of the terms and conditions under which a loan is made.

Commitment Letter—A letter from the lender that states the amount of the mortgage, the number of years to repay the mortgage (the term), the interest rate, the loan origination fee, the annual percentage rate and the monthly charges.

Common Elements—Refers to the property not owned outright by a condo or co-op owner, including common roadways, amenities, building structures, central utilities, etc.

Community Apartment—A development in which an undivided interest in land is coupled with the right of exclusive occupancy of an apartment.

Condominium—A form of home ownership that combines individual ownership of one's unit with shared ownership of common facilities.

Condominium Declaration—The document which legally establishes a condominium and which, together with the bylaws, contains conditions, covenants and restrictions governing the sale, ownership, use and disposition of property.

Condominium Plan—A plan consisting of a description and survey map of the condominium project and recorded documents evidencing title to the property, including the bylaws and other rules and regulations.

Condominium Unit—In a condominium project, this is what the individual owner actually owns, consisting of the space contained within the exterior walls of the surrounding structure.

Contingency—A condition which must be satisfied before a contract is legally binding.

Contract of Sale—The agreement between the buyer and seller on the purchase price, terms, and conditions of a sale. -

Conveyance—The document used to effect a transfer, such as a deed, or mortgage.

Cooperative—A form of ownership where a corporation holds title to all of the units and the common areas and individuals receive shares of stock in the corporation entitling them to exclusive rights of occupancy of a particular unit pursuant to a long-term "proprietary" lease.

Cooperative Interest—The combination of the cooperative ownership and occupancy rights, which represents interests that cannot be divided.-

Covenant—An undertaking by one or more parties to a deed.

Credit—The ability of a person to borrow money, or obtain goods with payments over time, as a consequence of the favorable opinion held by a lender as to the person's financial situation and reliability.

Credit Bureau—A company that gathers information on consumers who use credit and sells that information in the form of a credit report to credit lenders.

Credit History—A credit history is a record of credit use. It is comprised of a list of individual consumer debts and an indication as to whether or not these debts were paid back in a timely fashion or "as agreed." Credit institutions have developed a complex recording system of documenting your credit history. This is called a credit report.

Credit Report—A document used by the credit industry to examine an individual's use of credit. It provides information on money that individuals have borrowed from credit institutions and a history of payments.

Credit Score—A computer-generated number that summarizes an individual's credit profile and predicts the likelihood that a borrower will repay future obligations.

Creditworthy—One's ability to qualify for credit and repay debts.

Credit Report—A report detailing the credit history of a prospective borrower that's used to help determine borrower creditworthiness.

Debt—A sum of money owed from one person or institution to another person or institution.

Debt-to-Income Ratio—The percentage of gross monthly income that goes toward paying for your monthly housing expense, installment debts, alimony, child support, car payments, and payments on revolving or open-ended accounts such as credit cards.

Declaring the Plan Effective—The sponsor's statement that subscription agreements for at least the required number of apartments have been obtained to permit the building's conversion.

Deed—Legal document by which title to real property is transferred from one owner to another. The deed contains a description of the property, and is signed, witnessed, and delivered to the buyer at closing.

Deed of Trust—A legal document that conveys title to real property to a third party. The third party holds title until the owner of the property has repaid the debt in full.

Default—Failure to meet legal obligations in a contract, including failure to make payments on a loan.

Delinquency—Failure to make payments as agreed in the loan agreement.

Down Payment—The amount of a home's purchase price one needs to supply up front in cash to get a loan.

Earnest Money—Deposit made by a buyer towards the down payment in evidence of good faith when the purchase agreement is signed.

Equity—The difference between the current market value of a property and the total debt obligations against the property. On a new mortgage loan, the down payment represents the equity in the property.

Escrow—A transaction in which a third party acts as the agent for seller and buyer, or for borrower and lender, in handling legal documents and disbursement of funds.

Escrow Account—An account held by the lender to which the borrower pays monthly installments, collected as part of the monthly mortgage payment, for annual expenses such as taxes and insurance. The lender disburses escrow account funds on behalf of the borrower when they become due. Also known as Impound Account.

Escrow Agent—A person with fiduciary responsibility to the buyer and seller, or the borrower and lender, to ensure that the terms of the purchase/sale or loan are carried out.

Eviction Plan—A plan for the conversion of residential property to cooperative or condominium ownership which provides that non-purchasing tenants will be subject to eviction after the expiration of specific time periods set by law.

Fee Simple—Refers to the private ownership of real estate in which the owner has the right to control, use, and transfer the property at will.

Fixed-Rate Loans—Fixed-rate loans have interest rates that do not change over the life of the loan. As a result, monthly payments for principal and interest are also fixed for the life of the loan.

Flip Tax—A fee that is levied by the cooperative in return for waiving the co-op's right to purchase when a cooperative shareholder sells his or her share.

Flood Insurance—Insurance that compensates for physical damage to a property by flood. Typically not covered under standard hazard insurance.

Forbearance—The act by the lender of refraining from taking legal action on a mortgage loan that is delinquent.

Foreclosure—Legal process by which a mortgaged property may be sold to pay off a mortgage loan that is in default.

Good Faith Estimate—Written estimate of the settlement costs the borrower will likely have to pay at closing. Under the Real Estate Settlement Procedures Act (RESPA), the lender is required to provide this disclosure to the borrower within three days of receiving a loan application.

Governing Documents—The declaration and all other documents, such as bylaws, rules and regulations, articles of incorporation or articles of association, which govern the operation of the condominium association.

Grace Period—Period of time during which a loan payment may be made after its due date without incurring a late penalty. The grace period is specified as part of the terms of the loan in the Note.

Grantee—One who receives a conveyance of real property by deed.

Grantor—One who conveys real property by deed.

Gross Monthly Income—The income you earn in a month before taxes and other deductions. Under certain circumstances, it may also include rental income, self-employed income, income from alimony, child support, public assistance payments, and retirement benefits.

Hazard Insurance—Protects the insured against loss due to fire or other natural disaster in exchange for a premium paid to the insurer.

Home Inspection—A professional inspection of a home to review the condition of the property. The inspection should include an evaluation of the plumbing, heating and cooling systems, roof, wiring, foundation and pest infestation.

Homeowner's Insurance—A policy that protects you and the lender from fire or flood, which damages the structure of the house; a liability, such as an injury to a visitor to your home; or damage to your personal property, such as your furniture, clothes or appliances.

Housing Expense Ratio—The percentage of your gross monthly income that goes toward paying for your housing expenses.

Interest—Charge paid for borrowing money, calculated as a percentage of the remaining balance of the amount borrowed.

Interest Rate Cap—Consumer safeguards which limit the amount the interest rate on an ARM loan can change in an adjustment interval and/or over the life of the loan.

Internal Revenue Code §216—A section of the U.S. federal tax law that permits individual cooperative members to deduct mortgage interest and property tax on their income tax returns just like other homeowners do by allowing cooperative housing corporations to pass-through the mortgage interest and real property tax deductions to their stockholders on a pro rata basis.

Joint Liability—Liability shared among two or more people, each of whom is liable for the full debt.

Joint Tenancy—A form of ownership of property giving each person equal interest in the property, including rights of survivorship.

Land-Only Cooperative—In a land-only cooperative, only the land beneath the building(s) is owned on a cooperative basis. The individual homes are owned subject to lease on the land. Land-only cooperatives are rare except for mobile home park cooperatives or manufactured housing park cooperatives are almost always land-only cooperatives.

Late Charge—Penalty paid by a borrower when a payment is made after the due date.

Leasehold Cooperative—In a leasehold cooperative, the cooperative corporation owns the building, but leases the land.

Leasing Cooperative—In a leasing cooperative, the cooperative corporation does not own the property in which members reside but rather leases it from another entity.

Legal Description—A means of identifying the exact boundaries of land.

Lender—The bank, mortgage company, or mortgage broker offering the loan.

Liabilities—Your debts and other monetary obligations.

Lien—A legal claim by one person on the property of another for security for payment of a debt.

Limited-Equity Housing Cooperative—A cooperative where the by-laws limit the resale price of a membership/shares for the purpose of keeping the housing permanently affordable to incoming members.

Loan Application—An initial statement of personal and financial information required to apply for a loan.

Loan Application Fee—Fee charged by a lender to cover the initial costs of processing a loan application. The fee may include the cost of obtaining a property appraisal, a credit report, and a lock-in fee or other closing costs incurred during the process or the fee may be in addition to these charges.

Loan Origination Fee—Fee charged by a lender to cover administrative costs of processing a loan.

Loan-to-Value Ratio (LTV)—The percentage of the loan amount to the appraised value (or the sales price, whichever is less) of the property.

Maintenance Charges—Monthly payments made by shareholders in a cooperative corporation for the expenses of operating the building, including real estate taxes, mortgage payments, fuel and building employee salaries.

Management Agent—A firm or entity hired by the cooperative to manage the development. The relationship between the cooperative and the management agent is usually governed by a specific contract, called a management agreement. Not all cooperatives use a management agent. Some larger cooperatives hire a General Manager as an employee of the co-op, others are managed by the members themselves. However, most large co-ops use a management company.

Management Agreement—A contractual arrangement between the cooperative corporation and the firm hired to manage the cooperative's property, which outline the firm's responsibilities and compensation.

Management Plan—A specific plan of operations provided by a management agent to the cooperative, in substantially greater detail than that provided in the management agreement. The plan may be attached to the management agreement as a rider.

Manufactured Housing Park Cooperative—A manufactured housing park that is owned on a cooperative basis.

Market-Rate Housing Cooperative—A cooperative (1) financed with interest rates considered market rates and (2) with no restrictions on membership/share resale prices.

Member/Shareholder—An individual who owns a share or membership in a cooperative, also referred to as shareholders.

Membership Committee—A committee that reviews incoming members and approves or rejects their application based upon specific criteria set forth by the Board of Directors.

Mitchell-Lama Cooperatives—Limited equity co-ops, supervised by local government, providing affordable housing for middle-income residents.

Mortgage—A written instrument, duly executed and delivered, that creates a lien upon real estate as security for the payment of a specific debt.

Mortgage Banker—An individual or company that originates and/or services mortgage loans.

Mortgage Broker—An individual or company that arranges financing for borrowers.

Mortgage Insurance—Insurance with a guarantee that if an owner defaults on mortgage payments, the insurer (FHA/HUD/VA) will pay the lender the owed balance.

Mortgage Loan—A loan for which real estate serves as collateral to provide for repayment in case of default.

Mortgage Note—Legal document obligating a borrower to repay a loan at a stated interest rate during a specified period of time. The agreement is secured by a mortgage or deed of trust or other security instrument.

Mortgagee—The lender in a mortgage loan transaction.

Mortgagor—The borrower in a mortgage loan transaction.

Multifamily Development—Four or more units of housing in a single building.

Mutual Housing Association—A nonprofit corporation that develops, owns and/or manages, or assists cooperatives and other forms of non-profit resident-controlled housing.

Net Monthly Income—Your take-home pay after taxes.

Non-Eviction Plan—A plan for the conversion of a residential property to a cooperative or condominium ownership which provides that tenants may not be evicted for failure to buy their apartments.

Occupancy Agreement—The contract between the cooperative corporation and the member that sets the conditions for the right to occupy a particular unit. FHA co-ops and some other co-ops call this contract an occupancy agreement; others refer to it as a proprietary lease. It sets forth the rights and obligations of the member and the cooperative to each other.

Offer—A formal bid from the homebuyer to the home seller to purchase a home.

Personal Property—Property which is not real property, and which consists of things temporary or movable, such as refrigerators, stoves, or air conditioners.

PITI—Abbreviation for Principal, Interest, Taxes and Insurance, the components of a monthly mortgage payment.

Planned Community—A community in which individuals hold title to their own single family homes that are located within the development, and the common areas of the development—such as the grounds and play areas—belong to an incorporated homeowner association.

Presentation of the Plan—The date on which the final offering plan or black book is given to the tenants by the sponsor.

Principal—The amount of debt, not counting interest, left on a loan.

Private Mortgage Insurance (PMI)—Insurance to protect the lender in case you default on your loan, generally not required with conventional loans if the down payment is at least 20%.

Proprietary Lease—A document granting the long term exclusive right of possession and occupancy of a designated unit to the owner of a cooperative.

Proxy or Proxy Vote—An authorization of one person to act on behalf of another for voting purposes.

Purchase Agreement—Contract signed by buyer and seller stating the terms and conditions under which a property will be sold.

Real Estate—The land and all the things permanently attached to it.

RCM (Registered Cooperative Manager)—A professional designation for cooperative site managers who have successfully completed NAHC's Registered Cooperative Manager Program.

Red Herring—The proposed or preliminary offering plan of cooperative or condominium ownership which is submitted by the sponsor to the governing official and to tenants, and which is subject to modification.

Recognition Agreement—An understanding between a cooperative and a financial institution that provides share loans to the cooperative's members or shareholders.

Regulatory Agreement—An agreement which requires the co-op to abide by the regulations of HUD (or FHA), which insured the mortgage in order to induce a lender to finance the development. This document binds the mortgagor (the cooperative) and mortgagee (the financial institution that holds the mortgage until the amount borrowed, plus interest, is paid) with the Secretary of HUD.

Replacement Cost—The cost to replace damaged personal property without a deduction for depreciation.

Resale—The process of transferring a share from an outgoing co-op member to a new member.

Reserve—A fund set aside by the sponsor from the purchase price of the property for use by the cooperative corporation or condominium for future capital improvements or expenses, also referred to as a working capital fund.

RESPA—The Real Estate Settlement Procedures Act, a federal law that gives consumers the right to review information about loan settlement costs.

Right of First Approval—Most co-ops have a process to review and approve new members/shareholders. Your purchase of a membership/share is conditioned on the co-ops review and approval of your application and abilities to meet your obligations under the occupancy agreement. Co-ops may not discriminate against any protected class under local, state, and federal law.

Right of First Refusal—If a co-op's bylaws contain a right of first refusal clause, the co-op has the first option to purchase or refuse to purchase the outgoing member's share at an agreed upon price.

Right of Survivorship—The automatic succession to the interest of a deceased joint owner in a joint tenancy.

Right to Rescission—Under the provisions of the Truth-in-Lending Act, the borrower's right, on certain kinds of loans, to cancel the loan within three days of signing a mortgage.

Sales Agreement—Contract signed by buyer and seller stating the terms and conditions under which a property will be sold.

Section 203(n)—Program that insures loans for persons buying a share/membership in a housing cooperative.

Section 213—A HUD program that insures mortgages only on cooperative housing projects on a market rate basis.

Section 221(d)(3)—An HUD/FHA program that insures mortgages for the new construction or substantial rehabilitation of multifamily cooperatives and nonprofit rental housing.

Self-Management—In a self-managed cooperative, cooperative members perform the function of maintenance and administration themselves, or contract to various vendors.

Senior Housing Cooperative—Cooperatively owned or controlled housing designed especially for seniors.

Share—The proportion of the cooperative that each member owns, and it represents the proportionate amount that each member invested in the co-op when the co-op was started. A certificate, often called a stock or membership certificate, documents the purchase price and membership in the cooperative.

Shareholder—A shareholder, also called a member, is the owner of a share in a housing cooperative.

Share Loan—A loan obtained to purchase a share in a housing co-op secured by the shares and occupancy rights.

Site Manager—The individual who is employed by the cooperative or the cooperative's management agent to perform the necessary on-site management functions. The site manager may or may not reside on-site, and may or may not be employed full time.

Sponsor—The individual, partnership, corporation or other legal entity that offers to sell interests in a cooperative, condominium, timeshare or homeowners' association.

Statute of Frauds—Legal doctrine providing that all agreements concerning title to real estate must be in writing to be enforceable.

Stock Certificate—Documentation of ownership of share(s) in a cooperative, indicating the number of shares registered in the name of the owner.

Student Housing Cooperative—Located near colleges and universities, student housing cooperatives provide a variety of shared housing, dormitory arrangements, or apartments to meet student needs for low-cost housing.

Subchapter T—Subchapter T refers to Sections 1381 to 1388 of the U.S. Internal Revenue Code, which cover cooperatives that serve some public benefit.

Sublease—A lease between a current co-op shareholder and another person.

Subscription Agreement—The contract which constitutes the agreement by a purchaser to buy shares of stock in a cooperative corporation, or to purchase a condominium unit, also referred to as a purchase agreement.

Subscription Funds—Subscription funds are a fee or price paid along with the subscription agreement or purchase agreement.

Subsidized Housing Cooperative—A subsidized housing co-op receives a subsidy of some kind from the federal, state, or local government or other sources in order to lower the overall costs of the housing.

Survey—A measurement of land, prepared by a licensed surveyor, showing a property's boundaries, elevations, improvements, and relationship to surrounding tracts.

Tax Lien—Claim against a property for unpaid taxes.

Term—The period of time between the beginning loan date on the legal documents and the date the entire balance of the loan is due.

Title—Document which gives evidence of ownership of a property. Also indicates the rights of ownership and possession of the property.

Title Company—A company that insures title to property.

Title Insurance—Refers to an insurance policy which protects the lender and/or buyer against loss due to disputes over ownership of a property.

Title Search—Examination of municipal records to ensure that the seller is the legal owner of a property and that there are no liens or other claims against the property.

Transfer Tax—Tax paid when title passes from one owner to another.

Transfer Value—The dollar amount of the membership or share in a housing cooperative as set by the bylaws in event the cooperative repurchases the membership/share. In a limited equity co-op, the transfer value is the maximum amount at which a member's share in the co-op may be sold according to the co-op's limited equity formula.

Truth-in-Lending Act—Federal law requiring written disclosure of the terms of a mortgage by a lender to a borrower after application.

Underwriting—In mortgage lending, the process of determining the risks involved in a particular loan and establishing suitable terms and conditions for the loan.

U.S. Department of Housing and Urban Development (HUD)—A n agency within the U.S. government with chief administrative responsibility for providing a wide range of assistance for public and private housing and development of the nation's cities.

Usury—Interest charged in excess of the legal rate established by law.

Variable Rate—Interest rate that changes periodically in relation to an index.

Variance—The authorization to improve or develop a particular property in a manner not authorized by the zoning ordinance.

Verification of Employment (VOE)—Document signed by the borrower's employer verifying the borrower's position and salary.

Waiver—Voluntary relinquishment or surrender of some right or privilege.

Walk-through—A final inspection of a property to check for problems that may need to be corrected before closing.

Zoning Ordinances—Local law establishing building codes and usage regulations for properties in a specified area.

BIBLIOGRAPHY AND ADDITIONAL READING

Black's Law Dictionary, Fifth Edition. St. Paul, MN: West Publishing Company, 1979.

Findlaw (Date Visited: April 2005) <http://www.findlaw.com/>

Internal Revenue Service (Date Visited: April 2005) <http://www.irs.gov/>

The National Conference of Commissioners on Uniform State Laws (NCCUSL) (Date Visited: April 2005) <http://www.nccusl.org/>

Office of the New York State Attorney General Cooperative and Condominium Conversion Handbook. (Date Visited: April 2005) <http://www.oag.state.ny.us/realestate/conversion.html/>

The United States Department of Housing and Urban Development (Date Visited: April 2005) <http://www.hud.gov/>